KILLER ENGLISH: POSTMODERN THEORY AND THE CLASSROOM

Mary Alice Delia

ISBN: 979-8-9917187-0-7 (Paperback)

ISBN: 979-8-9917187-1-4 (Hardback)

ISBN: 979-8-9917187-2-1 (ebook)

A Brief Note to the Reader

Though written in the early 1990s, this book arrives at a moment when its central concerns are, if anything, more pressing than when it was first conceived. As the foreword makes clear, *Killer English* is not a relic of a passing theoretical moment; it is a sustained meditation on what it means to teach in a classroom shaped by language, power, and interpretation.

Readers interested in the book's personal history will find a dedication at the end of the volume. What remains is a living pedagogical argument—one addressed to teachers navigating the complexities of today's educational landscape.

Although the book centers on postmodern theory—engaging thinkers such as Jacques Derrida and Michel Foucault—its aim is neither abstraction nor allegiance to a theoretical camp. Its intention is practical and urgent: to cultivate deeper critical thinking, intellectual play, and imaginative risk in the classroom.

Many teachers understandably shy away from "theory," imagining it as distant from daily practice. Yet *every act of teaching already rests upon theory*—upon assumptions about knowledge, authority, language, and learning. Whether one subscribes to a model of transmission (knowledge delivered from expert to novice), construction (knowledge built through inquiry), or discipline (knowledge shaped by norms and power), *one is teaching from somewhere.*

As the author observes in the preface, theory has profoundly reshaped how we read texts, but far less often how we inhabit the classroom itself. This book invites educators to become conscious of the theories they already enact—and to consider how postmodern thought, used as one tool among many, can open spaces for ingenuity, reflection, and genuinely transformative learning.

March 2026

Mary Alice Delia

Mary Alice Delia

Contents

Mary Alice Delia

x

Foreword

In 1991, soon after joining the faculty at the University of Maryland, I had the good fortune to meet Mary Alice Delia and to accept the honor of serving as second reader for her extraordinary dissertation, "Killer English: Postmodern Theory and the Classroom." Agreeing to serve on that committee was one of the best academic decisions I ever made. Although I had experienced the challenges of teaching theory to undergraduates and had even written a article on that topic, Mary Alice exposed--without ever saying so--the narrow scope of my classroom innovations and my starched pedagogical timidity. I was captivated by her brilliant teaching strategies, which far exceeded my more limited and conventional practices. I was awed that she dared to teach postmodern theory in a high school setting at all, let alone through such dazzling inventiveness, and I was blown away by the signs of her success.

But *Killer English* is not just a "how-to" book, although it is rich in the best pedagogical strategies: it is a profound inquiry into postmodern thought. If the most intellectually radical classroom "remains stubbornly traditional in its attitude toward play," as Delia rightly charges, then we have missed postmodernism's most transformative theoretical points. *Killer English* offers the finest evidence that Foucauldian and Derridean thought, and postmodern theory in general, is itself profoundly pedagogical. To make her case, Delia doesn't just "do" pedagogy; she reads theorists like Derrida and Foucault *as* pedagogy, and in so doing she shows their contributions in a newer and truer light. And in a play-full one: as Delia observes, "the deconstructionist operation is not a treasure hunt for truth, at least not in the traditional sense of uncovering or discovering a truth-object. Instead, it tries, through graftings, parody, puns, and other textual plays, to multiple 'the outside in itself,' to increase the play of representation" (23).

Delia's own classroom texts are brilliant blends of conventional literary works--Shakespeare, Keats--and texts drawn from the students' own spheres, from official documents and letters to the editor to television shows and bridal registries, an array that helps students to see the underlying discourse rules of a particular genre or circumstance. As she writes, "If the present is, as Foucault believes, the story of power relations, and if power relations are embedded in every society, cultural, and institutional practice, then there is, in the present, no end to analysis and no shortage, ever, of discourse to look at" (101). The classroom itself becomes a text, as the students consider school codes as Foucauldian measure of discipline or analyze their own written excuses about missing class or doing shoddy work. *Killer English* describes a rich range of classroom moments in depth, providing detailed and adaptable practices for transforming student experience. She also shows how deftly designed group projects can yield far more than individual assignments in terms of learning that engages the students and lasts beyond the moment.

We are fortunate that although Delia wrote her book in the 1990s, her methodology is eminently transferable across grade levels, fields, and curricular priorities. Anyone who teaches humanities or qualitative social sciences, at whatever level and in whatever specialization, will find not only a powerful challenge in this book but pathways toward transforming your own classrooms and curricula. Delia's strategies have certainly found a place in my own classes, whether I have focused on prison narratives, apartheid South Africa, representations of women, or the French Revolution. Still, looking back on my career as I reread *Killer English,* I can see how hard one must work against the shopworn norms of the conventional classroom in which the teacher/expert holds forth before students that she hopes are listening. All the more reason to read and reread this book.

The adoption of an active pedagogy of the kind *Killer English* proposes has never been more urgent. At a time of precarious democracy and extraordinary threats to a culture of open inquiry, inclusion, and free thought, *Killer English* offers a path toward the kind of education for critical thinking that is so crucial to a democratic society. To be sure, the scope of "theory" has changed and grown since Mary Alice Delia wrote her book. But her strategies, deconstructive in the best and fullest sense, lend themselves beautifully to engage critical race theory, feminist and queer thought, postcolonialism, and indeed the spectrum of theoretical concerns that teachers bring to their engagement with students today. Mary Alice Delia's dissertation-turned-book is itself a classroom, a place for your own experimental engagement and deep learning. If you are a theorist, you will understand theory in a new way. If you are a teacher, at whatever academic level from elementary school through graduate students, you will find a myriad of ideas for teaching in new ways. And if you allow it, your classroom will never be the same.

Susan S. Lanser, Professor Emerita
Brandeis University
September 2024

Mary Alice Delia

Preface

Most readers would agree, I think, that postmodern theory, in the form of deconstruction and the new historicism, has made little difference in how we teach. Over the past thirty years, postmodern theory has altered the canon and transformed the way we read, but on the subject of teaching, it remains stubbornly silent. Rather than pursue its many implications for the classroom, post-modernism proceeds as though it has no classroom, as though its practice were a space constituted by the inquiry into the nature of language, truth, reality, self; a space structured by questions about language and the metaphysics of presence or by the interrogation of language and power relations.[1] The assumption seems to be "if we interpret a given literary text in a new way, we will undoubtedly teach it in a different way" (Cahalan and Downing 4), but if new readings guaranteed new practices, English classrooms all over the world would be making history. A theory of reading does not constitute a teaching practice; it is an ideological perspective that functions, in the classroom, as an agenda. And revolutionary though theory's new agendas may be, they have not, by and large, been accompanied by revolutionary new classroom practices.

This book will argue that postmodern theory has inescapable implications for pedagogy, at both the college and secondary level, and that the analysis of these implications is long overdue. Given prevailing attitudes toward pedagogy at the college level and toward theory at the secondary level, however, a book attempting to address both audiences is

---

[1] For an extended analysis of current writing on theory and pedagogy, see Cahalan and Downing's "Introduction," in *Practicing Theory...*, 2-16 and their excellent, annotated essay, "Selected Further Resources for Theory and Pedagogy: A Bibliographic Essay" in Practicing Theory...: 293-333. "Selected Further Resources ... groups pedagogical texts by theoretical orientation, e.g., cultural theory, psychoanalysis, feminism, multi-cultural theory. For a comprehensive bibliography of theory and pedagogy texts, see also the "List of Works Cited." [*Ed.*] For an updated review of the literature on postmodern research methodologies in education, see Campbell, M. (2018). Postmodernism and Educational Research. *Open Journal of Social Sciences*, 6, 67-73. For related discussions of the relationships between postmodern theory and pedagogy, see Tesar, M., Gibbons, A., Arndt, S., Hood, N. (2021). *Postmodernism in Education*. Available at: https://doi.org/10.1093/acrefore/9780190264093.013.1269; Garifullin, R. R. (2019) *Foundations of postmodern pedagogy*. Kazan Federal University; Burbules, N. C. (2009). Postmodernism and education. In S. Harvey (Ed.), *The Oxford Handbook of Philosophy of Education* (pp. 1-10). Oxford University Press.

bound to meet with resistance. For high school teachers, resistance will undoubtedly stem (reasonably enough, given constraints of money and time), from lack of knowledge about theory; for college teachers, from the long-standing perception of pedagogy as "secondary," or worse, as a non-issue.

In most college circles, as my own teaching experience suggests and as an anecdote related by Sharon Crowley affirms, the question of pedagogy is a question *in extremis*. Following a lecture by a noted critic on the need to politicize students, Crowley reports asking him "*how* he went about accomplishing the politicization of his students, in his classroom, every day" (emphasis mine.) The critic, Crowley writes, "was reluctant to answer my question and even seemed embarrassed for me. He apparently thought that by asking him for a lesson plan, or an account of what he does on Monday, I was demeaning myself (and him, by implication)" (25).

The critic's less-than-helpful response to Crowley's question is not surprising. For the most part, pedagogy, in *academe*, is deemed insufficiently rigorous for theoretical interrogation, a subject more appropriate for education departments than literary studies. Those who write about the classroom are not in the same intellectual "class" as those who write about theory. So strong is the academic bias against pedagogy as a legitimate subject of inquiry, that many college English teachers are *embarrassed* to talk about issues related to the classroom. Recently, I asked members of an electronic Derrida discussion group for ideas on how to introduce deconstruction theory to undergraduates. Not one "deconstructionist'' responded, not even privately. The silence was deafening and easily read: "We are on-line to discuss theory, not pedagogy!"

High school teachers, on the other hand, take pedagogical issues as their first priority. At the secondary level, the question of *how* to teach, *how* to introduce a novel or poem, receives more attention than issues relating to content or meaning. The *English Journal* is more interested in articles like "Using Poetry Cards to Stimulate Interest" or "How I Use Student Reading Groups to Teach Hamlet" than in questions and issues of interpretation. Although an ideal audience for publications pertaining to practice, high school English teachers profess themselves "put off" by postmodern theory. The ideas and concepts that now constitute literary studies in college, are viewed by many high school teachers with anxiety, skepticism, resentment, and, in some cases, outright hostility. Given adequate time, money, and support to access theory, most secondary teachers, I feel certain, will recognize its merits and experience a "change of heart." That scenario has not yet occurred, however, and meanwhile, practice in the high school classroom, as in the college classroom, continues as usual, unencumbered by theory and independent of its insights.

In the absence of a theorized pedagogy, teachers at all levels fall back on models of teaching provided by former professors and mentors (just as they, themselves, emulate the practices and styles of their own predecessors). Traditional pedagogies, no matter how elegant, cannot empower the insights students need to comprehend the complex texts of postmodern theorists such as Jacques Derrida and Michel Foucault.[2] What's needed is a new pedagogy capable of communicating theory's concepts and reflective of its values. Theory itself is rich in ideas for transforming the classroom and no one study can begin to suggest or exhaust the possibilities. This book explores (and limits discussion to) the possibilities of a pedagogy characterized by a postmodern understanding of play.

No one will deny that postmodern theory is difficult, time-consuming, and expensive to learn, but theory has become so integral a part of current academic talking and writing that theory, some might argue, is now what English is. That in time, theory's influence will extend to all levels of language study, kindergarten through postdoctoral, seems inevitable. Meanwhile, before the gap between theory and practice assumes the density of a black hole, we need to start talking and writing about the classroom, in publications, conferences, forums, seminars, colloquies, lectures, electronic discussion groups, speeches, wherever our many-leveled and culturally diverse voices are heard.

---

[2] Those who think undergraduate or secondary students do not need theory's insights or that postmodern theory is too difficult or too "problematic" for those just beginning the study of literature, will be persuaded otherwise, I hope, by arguments presented throughout this book. Derrida's own views on the role of philosophy in the *lycee* are well known. Asked in an interview if philosophy could be taught to a seventh grader, Derrida responded: "Among the so-called fundamental disciplines, why should philosophy be absent from secondary school education?" ("An Interview with Derrida" 78).

Mary Alice Delia

Introduction

Reality seemed slightly more intense at the playground. There was a dust, a daring. It was a children's world; nowhere else did we gather in such numbers with so few adults over us. The playground occupied a platform of earth; we were exposed, it seems now, to the sun and sky.

— John Updike, The Playground

I wish I could open this introduction by writing that at John Hopkins University in 1966, while delivering his famous lecture, "Structure, Sign, and Play in the Human Sciences," Jacques Derrida was hit *dead center* by a spitball. Alas, such a scene is unthinkable. One of the blind spots of postmodern theory is that it frees language to the play of interpretation but closes play off in its classroom. Without play, without risk, negotiation, exchange, the classroom is empty: what is supplemental to, absent, or lacking in it, cannot come *into* play. Of all postmodern values, it is play and its corollary, risk, that empower and transform the classroom, yet play is the one translation, the one invitation in theory that in practice, from the secondary classroom to the seminar, we are least open to.

Intellectually, we have moved beyond the idea of a fixed center to embrace play, but in the classroom, we lecture and carry on as though none of this play concerns or touches teaching, as though the performance were always elsewhere, in a text, and not where we are, in the classroom. Postmodern theory has reshaped the canon and redrawn the boundaries of literary study but in the classroom, it remains stubbornly traditional in its attitude toward play.[1] Walk down any corridor at 10:00 on a Monday morning and look in on an English classroom. Odds are the teacher is at

---

[1] [*Ed.*] Despite widespread recent discussions about the importance of a play-based approach to learning (for a conceptual analysis, see Parker, R., Thomsen, B. S., Berry, A. (2022). Learning Through Play at School – A Framework for Policy and Practice. *Front. Educ., 7*), the main claim of this manuscript remains still valid. The importance of play has been widely acknowledged in pedagogy and education theories but, in practice, the traditional ways of teaching and learning are still prevailing in the classroom, which does not leave much room for play (for an updated critical review of the effective practice of play-based learning in the classroom, see Bubikova-Moan, J., Hjetland, H. N., Wollscheid, S. (2019). ECE teachers' views on play-based learning: A systematic review. *European Early Childhood Education Research Journal, 27*, 776-800). Postmodern views of learning at every education level (but, in particular, in higher education) are no exception, and they confirm the gap between theory and practice when it comes to the role of play in the classroom.

the front of the room, talking; the students, at their desks, listening, perhaps taking notes. In the seminar, where play is talked about and where theory might be expected to effect a new and playful praxis, there is laughter perhaps, but as Derrida complains of Rousseau's festival, there is nothing to *see*.[2]

We cannot deny that the texts of postmodern theory are performative, or that "the grammatological attitude," as Said states, is "theatrical" (196). When we teach these texts in traditional, readerly ways, in lectures, teacher-centered discussions, or through reading assignments, we send a wrong message to students. We tell them, in effect, that our practice is less playful, less disruptive, less theatrical, than the theory that drives it. Traditional methodologies cannot communicate theory's most powerful performances: parodic interrogations, chiastic incursions, floodlit scenes, surgically detached operations, border transgressions, word genealogies, space/time acrobatics, graphic depictions of torture and dismemberment, and other postmodern maneuvers. Conventional classroom practices fail what in theory's texts seems most dramatic, most written, this book will argue, for the stage.

All this is not to suggest that we should dispense with lectures and reading assignments or take less seriously the business of teaching and learning theory: we should not. But surely, a theory which values difference compels us to think how to teach the difference of its own texts. And because theory's difference is constituted by a capacity for play we are obligated, it seems to me, to teach difference as playfully as we can. To that end, this book models techniques and strategies for introducing theory playfully, through props, demonstrations, scenes, stagings, and other performance-based activities.

For its theoretical framework, this book borrows heavily from the work of Gregory L. Ulmer,[3] the only scholar, to my knowledge, to deconstruct the work/play opposition and in so doing, to theorize a postmodern pedagogy. Ulmer has long insisted that the framing of the

---

[2] Current talk about play creates an impression of play, but this impression is a cruel illusion. In reality, the seminar, like the secondary and undergraduate classrooms, is empty of play. Perhaps it has always been so. But now, dominated by the abstractions of high theory and void of its performance, it is more so.
[3] [*Ed.*] For the latest developments of Ulmer's work, please see Ulmer, G. L. (2012). *Avatar Emergency*. Parlor Pr.; also see Ulmer, G. L. (2005). *Electronic Monuments*. University of Minnesota Press; Ulmer, G. L. (2003). *Internet Invention: From Literacy to Electracy*. Longman Pub Group.

scene of teaching is as important in a postmodern practice as the course content. *In Applied Grammatology: Post(e)-Pedagogy from Jacques Derrida to Joseph Beuys*, Ulmer analyzes the implications for pedagogy in Derrida's experimental (as opposed to philosophical) texts and in the practices of three postmodern teachers: Jacques Lacan, Joseph Beuys, and Sergei Eisenstein. Ulmer's analysis points to the concept of postmodern teaching as "a multimedia performance situation," one making use of scenes, experiments, invention, performance, nonverbal materials and apparatuses for demonstrations (*AP* 266).[4] The activities in this book owe much to Ulmer's call for a pedagogy that "*does* something *with* literature, rather than saying something about it" ("Textshop..." 45).

Because the chapters that follow "do things" with literature that are "so at odds with traditional English teaching" (as an early reviewer put it), some explanation of their content is called for. What sets the material in this book apart and makes special demands on the reader, is that the activities it introduces (the ducking of a rubber duck, the display of torture devices, the construction of a postmodern garden) are *not* activities normally seen in an English classroom. The difference of the material is distracting, and in some cases, frustrating; the reader may have difficulty comprehending the use of toys, gizmos, skits, and scenes in a classroom focused on "literature." It is the book's special and, in some ways, quite narrow argument, however, that what is done with theory in the classroom should be at least as radically transgressive as theory's performance in the text, e.g., Foucault's opening scene in *Discipline and Punish*, Derrida's use of columns and margins in "Tympan," Kristeva's fragmentations in "Stabat Mater," Bourdieu's dense mixture of discourses in *Distinction*.

Theory introduced playfully is not only more reflective of the spirit and value of postmodern inquiry, it is also easier to comprehend. Regardless of teaching level or course content, theory teachers share the difficulty of trying to teach, often in a too-short period of time, ideas that assume as their very point a certain "unteachability." Play, in the form of scenes, props, and stagings, helps students see and instantly apprehend what might otherwise take many lectures to communicate. The concept of depthlessness or anti-foundationalism, for example, is not only visualized but *experienced* when students play chess on a board suspended from the classroom ceiling on invisible wire. Whatever their age or background,

---

[4] As an introduction to Ulmer's ideas, I recommend "Text shop for Post(e)pedagogy," in *Writing and Reading Differently*.

students in the early stages of learning theory find the textual stage of theory's operations frustratingly abstract and distant from real life experience. The stagings that constitute "play" in this book are designed to help students draw closer, physically, to theory's performance on the page.

Stage

Because of the theoretical importance of the term stage to this book, its several meanings require elaboration. The archaic meaning of the word *stage*, one of two the book plays on, is "to furnish with a scaffold or platform" for public view. To stage postmodern theory in this sense of the word is to materialize and exhibit it, to put its views on view, to display, for contemplation, its concepts and ideas. The "raising" of issues for examination is of course a primary function of pedagogy, but in the traditional English classroom, it is done without recourse to the apparatus and machinery of the stage or platform. The question "Why don't we take a look at...?" *implies* some apparatus, object, action, to be observed, but falls short of producing it. A good staging makes a spectacle of itself; like any production, it makes dramatic use of props, machinery, movement, scenes, action.

The word *stage* also signifies "a period or step in a process, activity or development." This meaning, stage as learning *step*, is critical to theories of developmental learning and thus important to readers of this book. Most undergraduates, according to Widick, Knefelkamp, and Parker, are in the early, dualistic stages of cognitive development; they need a practice which challenges them intellectually but which is st(aged), one that takes into account the qualitative difference of their learning stages. In the early stages of development, students are less able to deal with theory in the abstract; they need learning experiences that are hands-on and concrete (292). The appropriate pedagogical practice for these students, as Widick et al point out, is experiential, one that makes use of tangible objects and that provides in-class opportunities to tinker and "test-out" perceptions (291).

Because the performance or staging-model of theory encourages risk, is hands-on and experiential, it is especially appropriate for undergraduates and, I would argue, for all students beginning a new and rigorous course of study, regardless of age. (One finds few relativists in "Introduction to Microbiology.") With the two meanings of the word *stage* in mind, then, the challenge is to transform theory's abstractions into scenes or performances that students new to theory can experience physically and enter *into*. The project is not for the fainthearted. For traditional or relatively inexperienced teachers, the leap from the text to the stage—from the discussion of a complex theoretical idea to a performance that makes use of bodies and objects—will be a bit scary. But students respect the willingness to risk and for the most part, respond positively.

The Invitation to Play

If we can agree that students benefit from the staging of theory, the practical question—and one central to this book— is how to bring the stage *into* the classroom, how to think and shape the moves that summon it. Recently, for a workshop comprised of chiefly of non-English teachers, I was asked to prepare a lesson demonstrating the difference between a traditional approach to teaching a poem and a "postmodern" approach.[5] For a text, I chose Frost's "Stopping by Woods on a Snowy Evening," a poem that opens easily to post-modern analysis.

Following a reading of the poem by one of the participants, I suggested that some postmodernists might argue that Frost feminizes the woods by depicting the trees as *femmes fatales* or entrapping sirens. One student, a biology teacher and football coach, shook his head incredulously. "Maybe I just don't understand poetry," he objected, "but I can't see it."

One strategy for helping students "see" the post-modern critique is to enact the reading as a dramatization.[6] To show the feminist view of the

---

[5] By "postmodern," "I mean those theories that follow modernism chronologically and are united in their attack on the modernist concept of literature as an autonomous art object subject to its own epistemology or "way of knowing." In this book, the term *post-modern* includes (but is not limited to) poststructual theory (deconstruction, new historicism), feminism, psychoanalysis, queer, lesbian, gay theory, and all theories that reject, categorically, the idea of a structured center.

[6] [*Ed.*] The use of dramatization in reading is consistent with the enactment theory, which has been introduced by Weik (Weick, K. E. (1988). Enacted sensemaking in crisis situations. *Journal of Management Studies, 24*(4)) and developed during the 90s and 20s in different fields. The use of enactment as a pedagogical tool has became particularly popular recently in studies on narrative comprehension (see, for example, Poeckl, C. V. (2021). The Literature-Enactment-Process. Exploring narratives through performative conventions. *Scenario, 15*(1)), also thanks to the influence of the "embodied cognition" theory, according to which language comprehension and thought involve processes also involved in actions, perceptions, and emotions (see the seminal article by Barsalou, L. W.

woods as "entrapping sirens," I asked the women participants to stand together in the manner of a stand of trees and to move their arms through the air like branches swayed by an "easy wind." Then, to give the coach both a role and a *stake* in the reading, I provided him with a yardstick "horse" and asked him to ride by the "lovely, dark and deep" woods. Being a good sport, he did so and as he approached the "woods," I asked the women, also good sports, to make soft, whispery cries and clutching, pulling motions with their hands. Recoiling half in fun and half in earnest, the coach hurried his "little horse" past the tree-sirens and right out the classroom door! "A good scene," Ulmer reminds us, is always better than "a long discourse" and a good horse, of course, always makes a good scene (*AG* 266).

Other stagings begin with an idea for an apparatus, a "thingamajig," contrivance, device, or object that powerfully embodies a theoretical idea. The effect of such an apparatus is a radical cynosure, an excited turning to the idea-on-display, a "sudden rush" of recognition. A good apparatus draws the eye, but it also makes the heart race and if excellent, the hair stand straight up on end. To prepare the reader in advance, I show and comment on one such apparatus here.

To introduce the disciplinary mechanism(s) that Foucault, writing in *Discipline and Punishment*, finds at the heart of all institutional discourse, I contracted with two students to construct, for the classroom, a full-size, working gallows consisting of a raised platform (with operating trap door) and an upright post (braced with 2x4's), complete with crosspiece and heavy rope noose. On the appointed day, the students arrived in the room to find the chairs pushed aside and the gallows dead center. Their eyes opened wide in astonishment.

"Whaaaa...?"

"Ohmigod."

"Where did *this* come from?"

(1999). Perceptual symbol systems. *Behavioral and Brain Sciences, 22*, 577–660; for recent reviews and overviews, see Shapiro, L., & Spaulding, S. (2021). Embodied Cognition. *The Stanford Encyclopedia of Philosophy*, Edward N. Zalta (ed.); Zwaan, R. A. (2021). Two Challenges to "Embodied Cognition" Research and How to Overcome Them. *Journal of Cognition, 4*(1), 14; Shapiro, L. (2019). *Embodied Cognition 2nd Edition*. Routledge).

"From this very room," I said. "The gallows has always been in the classroom. The reason you have not seen it is that about two hundred years ago, it disappeared from view. It went underground, so to speak. And when it reappeared, it took a different form. It now looks like this." I picked up and displayed a familiar school publication, the "Student Discipline Code."

"COOL!" Wheels turned, eyes flew, some straight to the gallows, other from the gallows to the discipline code. two students tried to hang themselves. All had ideas and questions.

"I'm next."

"Does the administration know about this?"

"Could someone really die on this thing?"

"What do you mean 'underground'? Underground where?"

"How can a gallows turn into a book?"

"Could you get fired for this?"

These questions and others served as a highly effective pretext for linking ideas in Foucault's *Discipline and Punish* with events in Kesey's *One Flew Over the Cuckoo's Nest* and Hawthorne's *The Scarlet Letter*. Discussions of *these* readings, led, in turn, to the construction of postmodern Barbie dolls; the invention of several in carceral apparatuses, including a working rack; and, among other projects, a Foucauldian discourse establishing micro penalties for delinquent joggers (projects shown in Chapter 3).[7]

---

[7] Some readers may find the "non-literary" aspects of this project problematic but the real problem, as Ulmer sees it, is the failure to deconstruct the distinction between literary and nonliterary and between the formal essay and all other forms and modes of inscription. As teachers, Ulmer observes, we have been trained in the "analytical, calculative paradigm of reason"; we are open to new ideas- *providing* they are presented to us in "the familiar expository form of literary criticism" (114-116). [*Ed.*] To reinforce this point, note that the difficulty to distinguish between "literary" and "non-literary" aspects has very deep roots, which go beyond its discussion in literary and narrative studies. One of the sources of such difficulty lies in the language use itself (spoken and written) and the distiction between "pragmatics" and "semantics." While the latter concerns the meaning of words (intended as a mental lexicon) and sentences (intended as the result of the rule-based combination of words), the former concerns the context (linguistic and extra-linguistic) in which words and sentences are interpreted. For a recent general discussion, see Depraetere, I., & Salkie, R., eds. (2017). *Semantics and Pragmatics: Drawing a Line.* Springer.

The Audience & Chapter Contents

Before concluding with a description of chapter contents, I want to comment, once more, on issues relating to the book's boundaries, limitations, and intended audience. Although addressed primarily to teachers of secondary students and undergraduates, this book should be useful to any teacher faced with the challenge of introducing, in a short period of time, the concepts and vocabularies of postmodern theory. While I assume the book's readers have some knowledge of postmodern theory, I have tried, where possible, to provide brief explanations of the "theory behind the scene." Some readers will find this background information insufficient; others may find it distracting or offensively simplistic. Other than to acknowledge the problem, I can do little but beg forbearance, both of those who want more and of those who want less.

I am aware, also, that while some readers may see the immediate relevance of the materials in this book for their own practice, others will want more contextualization or suggestions for fitting the scenes and demonstrations into a specific curriculum. The latter will want to know what happens after (or before) the scenes, if for example, after playing chess in midair, students go on to the hard work of reading "Structure, Sign, and Play." In response I will say that some classes go on to read theory, others may not, depending on factors unique to the class situation. I do understand the need for specific suggestions and I try, albeit in a limited way, to respond appropriately. Regardless of my effort to give the reader a clear understanding of the book's audience and limitations, I am certain to have overlooked aspects of the book that should, in this introduction, have been given consideration. Perhaps, in the overview of the chapters which follows this section, the reader will find answers to concerns and issues not yet addressed.

With regard to the description of chapter contents, I have two important concerns. For one, I do not want readers to infer from the descriptions that because I encourage play, I have abandoned all traditional activities and assignments. I have not. In a postmodern practice, play and work are not oppositional; play does not displace reading, writing, and thinking about literature in ways that are intellectually rigorous (although one effect of play is that students enjoy the work more and invest more in the task). In a typical semester, for example, my students might read and discuss *Their Eyes Were Watching*

God, *One Flew Over the Cuckoo's Nest*, *Song of Solomon*, *The Tempest*, *The Scarlet Letter*, *Life in the Iron Mills*, *Trifles*, *Sula*, and *A Streetcar Named Desire* as well as selections from feminist criticism and the texts of Derrida and Foucault.

I am also concerned that because I am more interested, in this book, in showing scenes rather than dross spots, demonstrations rather than lectures, props rather than texts, my practice may appear to be more playful than it actually is. As I am sure my reader suspects, not all my class sessions are *jouissant*; some roll merrily along; others, apathetic and lackluster.

Underlying each of the book's five chapters is the idea that aspects of postmodern theory, when translated into developmentally appropriate classroom activities, can help secondary and undergraduate students understand language as a site of struggle. Chapters 1 and 2 are devoted to Derrida and deconstruction theory. Chapter 1 contains techniques for introducing Derrida's attack on logocentrism, or the privileging of speech over writing. It also provides two scripts, one for a performance of a feminist-deconstructionist reading of Keat's "Bright Star" and one for a deconstructionist demonstration lesson on *Hamlet* (along with student responses and critiques). Chapter 2 offers activities and materials for interrogating alphabetic and non-alphabetic writing. It offers suggestions for writing projects that make use of homonymic play, ideas for the construction of postmodern apparatuses, and directions for planting "a garden of postmodern delights."

Chapters 3 and 4 are devoted to Foucault and new historicist theory. Chapter 3 contains activities and materials for introducing culture as a concept. It makes a case for the school as a first object of new historicist inquiry; provides schoolrelated materials for analysis, along with materials linking school discourse with discourse from other domains of student interest; and proposes techniques and activities for combining analysis with illustration. Chapter 4 contains materials and strategies for the analysis of power relations and for approaching the literary text as discourse. It models a new historicist research project framed as an investigative report; shows examples of new, experimental project report styles; argues for the displacement of the student journal with the letter; and suggests strategies for interrogating the letter both as writing and as discourse.

Chapter 5 examines the role of props in the postmodern classroom and provides an annotated list of props tested in my own practice. Props, as this chapter suggests, provide powerful tools for piquing student interest in theory and for effecting perceptual breakthroughs. The props described in this chapter are not prescriptive; they intend only to argue the value of the apparatus in the postmodern classroom, to suggest that in the same way theory breaches textual boundaries, practitioners of theory must now breach "the classroom supply list," reaching everywhere- into toy stores, kitchens, garage sales, antique shops, tool boxes- for new pedagogical materials. As this chapter argues, even the materials found traditionally in the classroom (chalk, eraser, blackboard) can and should be put to postmodern uses. Theory supplies the logic of play, but the apparatus of play, the equipment, gadgets, and gaming pieces, are the domain of the classroom.

I conclude this introduction by circling back to its opening text, the passage taken from John Updike's essay, "The Playground." Outside my classroom is a playground used by the school's early education program. I have only to look out the window to see the "daring" that characterizes it and that for Updike, intensifies reality. A child runs screaming in a circle, eyes shut tight. Another shoots down a slide on his back, headfirst. Another hides himself in a bush. Terms are negotiated; possessions exchanged, substituted or simply wrenched away. Expressions of glee, surprise, delight change, in the twinkle of an eye, to expressions of anger, indignation, frustration, denial. Authority is not absent from the playground, but it is less evident there: children interact freely, wiggle bodies, test limits, try out ideas, pop out of bushes, strike deals. Seen through the lens of theory, the playground would appear to be the ideal postmodern classroom, a space open to risk, mask, daring, death, negotiation, dance, contestation, and beyond that, to the "the sun and the sky," a platform or stage for exhibit, {dis}play, and exposure.

CHAPTER ONE
Introducing Aspects of Deconstruction Theory

> *One misty, moisty morning,*
> *When cloudy was the weather,*
> *I chanced to meet an old man clothed all in leather.*
> *He began to compliment, and I began to grin,*
> *How do you do, and how do you do?*
> *And how do you do again?*

> — Mother Goose

In the Preface to *Of Grammatology*, a primer of deconstruction theory,[1] Derrida provides an uncharacteristically clear guide to the book's organization: the first part "proposes certain critical concepts"; the second part puts these concepts "to the test" (lxxxix). The organization of this chapter follows that of Derrida's: the first section focuses on concepts and background critical to deconstruction theory; the three sections following explore the implications of these concepts for a playful (performative) pedagogy.

The demonstrations, scenes, and activities in the first section are designed, in part, to demystify deconstruction and to assure students that an understanding of its terms and concepts is well within their grasp. The focus is on Derrida's attack on the privileging of speech over writing (logocentrism) and on his argument that writing subsumes speech. Because perceptual breakthroughs are more apt to accompany exercises that are experiential rather than abstract, the activities in this section (as throughout the book) are performative in nature, i.e., they make use of

---

[1] Because of the importance of *of Grammatology* to the first two chapters of this book, I strongly recommend reading (at very least) the following sections: "The End of the Book and the Beginning of Writing," "Linguistics and Grammatology," and "Of Grammatology as a Positive Science." [*Ed.*] First published in 1967 (Derrid, J. (1967). *De la grammatologie*. Paris: Les Éditions de Minuit), the book was translated in English as *Of Grammatology* by Gayatri Chakravorty Spivak and first published in 1976 by Johns Hopkins University Press. Since its translation in English, many commentaries have appeared that tried to explain and discuss the philosophical problems addressed in this relevant book. Among those, I recommend *Reading Derrida's of Grammatology* (Gaston, S., & Maclachlan, I. (eds.) (2011). *Reading Derrida's Grammatology*. Continuum), which offers an overview on the most influential takes on Derrida's book as of 2011.

games, pantomime, role-playing, demonstrations, and other participatory exchanges.

The second section features a deconstructionist-feminist reading of Keats' sonnet "Bright Star," staged as a murder mystery in two scenes. In this Columbo-inspired script, students observe the deconstructive operation and also, the importance of deconstruction's tools to feminist criticism (and other postmodern critiques). The third and longest section, a deconstructionist lesson on *Hamlet* presented to a class of undergraduates (role-played here by seminar students), provides an idea of what a practice driven by deconstruction might look like. Although a bit fast-paced for undergraduates as staged, the *Hamlet* lesson models strategies for constructing and deconstructing in the same operation, the challenge of a self-reflexive pedagogy. Intended in part as a response to Sharon Crowley's[2] question: "What do you [a postmodern teacher] do on Monday morning?," the *Hamlet* lesson also shows "the good things that happen" in the classroom when deconstruction is taken, in Susan Handelman's[3] words, as an "invitation to a *performative* mode instead of a constant intellectual worrying over uncertainty and aporia."[4]

The final section contains excerpts from the seminar students' critiques of the *Hamlet* demonstration lesson, followed by my own comments and observations. The critiques and comments provide insight into deconstruction theory as well as a forum for debating the "pros and cons" of introducing deconstruction in the undergraduate or secondary classroom. As I am certain the reader knows, many teachers consider Derrida's texts too difficult and/or too epistemologically shocking, for students in lower-level courses. Proponents of Derrida's theories, on the other hand, contend that deconstruction is not an advanced, late-stage

---

[2] [*Ed.*] Sharon Crowley is professor of professor of rhetoric and composition at Arizona State University. She has written articles on the history of rhetoric and composition and on postmodernism in the teaching of writing. She is the author of *Composition in the University, The Methodical Memory,* and the textbook *Ancient Rhetorics for Contemporary Students.*

[3] [*Ed.*] Susan Handelman is a professor of English at Bar-Ilan University in Israel. She has published many books and articles on the relation of Jewish thought and literature, academia and spirituality, including *The Slayers of Moses: The Emergence of Rabbinic Interpretation in Modern Literary Theory*; *Fragments of Redemption: Jewish Thought and Literary Theory in Scholem, Benjamin and Levinas*; *Make Yourself a teacher: Rabbinic Tales of Mentors and Disciples.*

[4] Letter to the author. November 5, 1987.

operation on a literary text but a first operation on language and one that should be learned even as students learn to read.

Section 1: The Critique of Logocentrism

Platonism and "The Allegory of the Cave[5]"

For most students, an introduction to Derrida means coming to terms with his attack on "logocentrism": the privileging, in western thought, of speech over writing, the valorization of presence over absence.[6] A full account of Derrida's critique is beyond the scope of this book, but briefly, Derrida argues that from Plato through Hegel, for reasons that have no demonstrable basis in fact and are thus "metaphysical," the written word has always been assumed inferior or secondary to *logos*, "the living word," or speech. In the same way that Coffeemate must sometimes substitute for cream, writing substitutes for speech, but as any coffee purist will attest, Coffeemate will never take the place of cream. Cream, after all, is the "real thing."

In the past, the assumption has been that words spoken are nearer, more present to the speaker's real "self" than graphite marks on a page, that words spoken embody a presence or life that writing lacks, that speech is in intimate, interior relation to the word whereas writing is exterior and therefore unconnected to the word. Writing (re)presents reality through signs that are subject to distortion; speech, on the other hand, opens directly onto truth or reality. Writing is the *absence* of speech; it has no "inside"; it does not issue from the mouth but from the hand, and the hand, as Derrida writes, has long been regarded as forgetful, sly, tricky, manipulative.

---

[5] [*Ed.*] Plato's "Allegory of the Cave" was developed to discuss the nature of belief versus knowledge. In the allegory, prisoners live chained in a cave all their lives. A fire burns behind the prisoners, and between the fire and the prisoners are people carrying dolls or other objects that cast shadows on the opposite wall. The prisoners believe that these shadows are their reality, for they have known nothing else. Plato imagines that a prisoner becomes free, sees the fire and realises that the shadows are not real. This prisoner is able to escape from the cave and discovers that there is a whole new world outside that they have never known before. The prisoner would believe that the world outside is so much more real than the one in the cave. Thus, the prisoner returns to free the other prisoners, but he is blinded because his eyes are not used to the real sunlight. The chained prisoners see this blindness and believe that they will be harmed if they try to leave the cave.
[6] See "Writing Before the Letter," Part I of *of Grammatology*, pp. 6-93.

In his critique of Plato, Derrida deconstructs the longstanding speech/writing opposition.[7] It is Derrida's argument that writing does not oppose speech but subsumes it, that speech, is itself, a form of writing. The *desire* to signify, Derrida argues, should not lead us to imagine that the spoken word is more real, more material, than the word that is written. Derrida argues that like writing, speech depends on the use of signs, differentiation, spacing, intervals and substitutions to produce meaning. Like writing, speech is subject to the order of language, grammar, syntax. For Derrida, not only speech but *all* "that gives rise to inscription"– painting, music, sculpture, sports, films–is writing (*OG* 9). For Derrida, there is, in fact, "no linguistic sign before writing" (*OG* 14).

The effect of Derrida's attack on logocentrism is to focus the spotlight on language as the sole constructor of knowledge, truth, reality. Derrida's point, of course, is that language is empty, that despite its attempt to signify a reality outside of itself, it cannot produce knowledge of anything except of itself, as language. Knowledge of self does not exist outside of the order of language and if the self is constituted by language, Derrida argues, then we should look, really *look* at language, not as a window onto the self or as a saran wrap for Truth, but as a linguistic system subject to its own rules and order of play. Whereas new historicist theory[8] looks at language for clues to cultural and social practices, Derrida looks at the way language tries to conceal its emptiness, its inability to signify reality, truth, meaning. Like other postmodernists, Derrida views language as the site of struggle and like others, tries to keep language open, not, like new historicism, to issues of power, but to the play of signification or representation. For Derrida, the text is a labyrinth from which the only exit is the entrance to another text.

How to introduce the study of linguistic play, signs substituting for signs in a field without closure, is the subject of the following sections;

---

[7] Deconstruction questions the hierarchical structures of all conceptual oppositions; its method is to expose the metaphysical bias (ethnocentrism, self) underlying the privileging of one term over the other, the left over the right. In addition to speech/writing are mind/body; presence/absence; theory/practice; nature/culture; content/form; meaning/expression; literal/figurative (Crowley 12). The following oppositions also undergo Derrida's critique: life/death, father/son, master/servant, first/second, legitimate/orphan, soul/body, inside/outside, good/evil, seriousness/play, day/night, sun/moon, remedy/poison, intelligible/sensible, high/low, mind/matter .... (*Diss* 24, 85)

[8] For an overview of new historicist theory, see the introduction to Chapter 3. [*Ed.*] New Historicism is a literary theory based on the idea that literature should be studied and interpreted in the context of both the author's and the critic's history.

the focus here is on activities for introducing the concept of logocentrism, or the privileging of presence. Obviously, these activities, many of which are quite brief, cannot displace the hard work of reading Derrida, but they help demystify theory and prepare students for the challenge of reading it. Although the critique of logocentrism informs all of Derrida's work, students, in my experience, find it most accessible in Part I of *of Grammatology*, a text Sharon Crowley finds "central to the work of English teachers" and, I would add, to the classroom (50).[9] Rather than reserve this text for teachers, I recommend using it (in whole or in part, as time, money, and energy permit) as a text, in the classroom. On the stage of Derrida's critique, why should his own performance, in *of Grammatology*, be absent?

Activities for Introducing the Concept of Logocentrism

The Critique of Plato

As observed earlier, Derrida opens his attack on logocentrism by deconstructing the platonic idea that speech and writing are oppositional and that writing is inferior to speech. To set the scene for Derrida's attack, invoke the discourse of philosophy. Bring Plato on stage as a character in a narrated pantomime of "The Allegory of the Cave." To hint at the cave's dangers and to invite play, distribute several pairs of "snake boots" and scatter around a few stones and rubber bats.

"Spelunking with Socrates"

Characters & Props:

Socrates (in academic robe)
Plato (in academic robe)
Glaucon (in robe)
Prisoners chained in the cave
Students carrying objects
Students with flashlights
Enlightened prisoner
Pen and paper

Directions: Darken the room, seat four or five prisoners on the floor facing a wall and chain their arms and legs together. Direct students

---

[9] Teachers unfamiliar with Derrida's work will find Sharon Crowley's suggestions for reading Derrida quite helpful. See especially pages 49-50 in *A Teacher's Guide to Deconstruction*.

carrying objects (gathered from the room) to walk back and forth behind the prisoners. Station students with flashlights behind those carrying objects, so that the shadows of the objects will be cast on the wall in front of the prisoners. Have Socrates and Glaucon read aloud "The Allegory of the Cave" while the "enlightened" prisoner silently enacts it. Seat Plato at a desk with instructions to record the dialogue.

The staging of Plato's text shows, among other things, how a philosophical concept can be enacted as a performance students can enter into. Performance provides a living framework for discussion, in this case, of the idea of permanent, fixed forms or truths, and, grist for Derrida's mill, the idea of language as originating in a first word, a living word, the word of a God whose presence is guaranteed by the blinding light of the sun. In "The Allegory of the Cave," Plato argues that the sun is a living God and it is this God who speaks, gives breath to, and guarantees the word. God's word is *logos*, the living word, the highest reality. But for Derrida, the association of language with the sun is, as Said puts it, a strategy for blinding oneself to writing (193).

Perceiving Plato's Proposition as Writing

Derrida's argument that writing *subsumes* speech, that speech is itself a form of writing, is difficult for students to grasp. Derrida attacks Plato's argument by observing that the argument is itself, written, and therefore, subject to Plato's own critique. Presented as dialogue, Plato's writing "looks" like speech, but its first reality, according to Derrida, is writing. To help students comprehend Plato's argument as writing, show it as writing. Before students arrive for class, write in tiny script on a remote, hard-to-see section of the wall, Plato's proposition: "Writing imitates speech." Open class with the question: "What is this proposition of Plato's: 'Writing imitates speech'"?[10]

The deconstructionist response to Plato's question is language or writing, but the students' "seeing" of Plato's proposition literally as *writing*, may be a long time coming, perhaps an entire class hour. Students will take the question as an invitation to interpret and will proceed to puzzle out its meaning. The teacher's role is to reject each

---

[10] To show pedagogy as the act of fishing for an answer, sit on the edge of your desk holding a fishing pole, hook, line, and sinker.

interpretation with a firm shake of the head. Eventually, the students will fall silent and wait for the teacher to come to her senses.

At that point, the teacher should offer a proposition of her own. "Let's find that question and take a look at it."

The teacher should then wander about the room, searching under books, in coat pockets, behind the door, on the floor. Students will join in and eventually, the proposition will be found and identified as *writing*. My own students needed a little help.

"Here it is!"

"What is 'it'?"

"The proposition!"

"That's what you say it is. What would a maintenance worker call it? Someone summoned to clean up the room?"

"Scribbling!"

"Graffiti!"

"Writing on the wall!"

The scene showing Plato's proposition as writing will stay with students and prepare them to understand Derrida's larger claim for writing as "all that gives rise to an inscription in general," voiced or unvoiced (*OG* 9).

The Critique of Presence

To loop the concept of logocentrism or the privileging of presence through the students' own prior language experiences, I ask them to brainstorm words and phrases which show the association of the spoken word or presence with truth or reality. Examples might include: "I got it from the horse's mouth"; "She told me in person"; "Those were her very words"; "Straight from the source" or "I hear you!" Students might also consider the privileging of presence in courtroom practices (the calling and "swearing in" of witnesses, the finger pointed in identification); in ceremonies such as marriage (Repeat after me: "Do you, Robert, take this woman...?"); in legal procedures such as notarization or deposition-taking; and in academic discourse.

Despite the fact that much academic language privileges presence over absence, academic language itself is rarely subject to critique.[11] Rather than ignore or disregard logocentric practices in the classroom, a self-reflexive pedagogy will identify and deconstruct them. In the language constituting the following attendance policies, for example, the privileging of presence is manifest:

> Class attendance is extremely important and is required. For each class you miss, you must submit a five-page paper based on an outside reading.
>
> Saint Louis University, 1993.
>
> You are expected to attend every class session. Failure to attend regularly will result in a failing grade.
>
> James Madison University, 1993.

After the analysis of assumptions underlying the above policies,[12] I try to show students their own assumptions about presence and absence, speech and writing. To bring their ideas center, I ask them to agree or disagree with the following statements:

> We are more present to ourselves when we speak.
>
> Speech penetrates; writing does not.

Most students agree with the statements. The assumption that speech penetrates, that it opens onto an interior self-writing has no access to, is deeply ingrained in our thinking and not easily deconstructed. Pedagogically, the challenge is to render the abstract concrete, to turn the classroom into a laboratory for testing the students' assumptions about language.

---

[11] Most papers and accouncements pertaining to academic routines, policies, and practices lend themselves readily to the deconstructive critique. Nowhere, for example, is the valorization of presence more pronounced than in the ritual of the orals, in which a candidate for an advanced degree is presented to a committee for examination. In conferences, a paper presented *in absentia* is considered less than full: it is not *logos, word*, but writing or representation.

[12] The attendance policy can also be subjected to Foucault's analysis of the disciplinary structures (micropenalties) at the heart of institutional discourse.

Up Against the Wall

In the following activity, an exercise in voice-throwing, the idea of a "living speech" is given a reality check. Line half the class up against one wall of the classroom and the other half, on the opposite wall, so that each student directly faces another and so that the two students operate as a team. Instruct the students along one wall to attack or "hit" the student directly across the room with the word *blue*, to shape and project the word so that it penetrates the student right between the eyes. (Students who miss the target should move two or three steps into the room, repeating the "step off" as necessary.) Points are scored when the student on the receiving end of the word confirms the "hit." The first pair of students to accumulate ten points wins the game and a fistful of blue M&M's.

The exercise would *seem* to substantiate the idea that sound and breath are unified, that speech is a connected, living, extension of self, that speech can penetrate and thus signify self. Originating from the interior, speech promises verisimilitude, essence, being. In reality, of course, the exercise confirms the inability of speech to signify self. In his critique of Plato, Derrida argues that the word and the breath (self, interior) are *not* unified; that speech is *not* connected to self; that speech *cannot* signify self. Although shaped by living lips and produced by living breath, words themselves have no materiality and regardless of how powerfully projected, they cannot penetrate, alter, or intensify reality. In the following account of a classroom demonstration, the idea of *logos* as "living word" is put to death.

The *Breathalyzer Test*

To start the demonstration, I asked the students to pant heavily into the palms of their hands. "Cup and feel the materiality of your breath," I said. "Feel its essence, its warmth." The students complied.

"Now, breathe the word *blue* into the cup of your hand." The students complied. I asked them to continue breathing *blue* until they felt or experienced a unity of word and breath, until the expelling of the word and the expelling of the breath seems to occur simultaneously.

I then asked: "The word *blue* seems one with the breath, exits right along with the breath, but is the word identical with the breath? Are the word and the breath one and the same?"

9

The students considered. Finally, most shook their heads. "What *is* the 'word' then?"

"The word, according to Derrida, is ...

"No! Let me guess. It's writing, right?"

Poster Collages

As a follow-up to the discussion of logocentrism and as a pretext for a postmodern project, I use the text of Adrienne Rich's "Tear Gas," a poem that speaks to the human desire for a language that is tangible, palpable, the hunger for" .... a word that will shed itself like a tear/ onto the page / leaving its stain/ "(*The Fact*...199). To signify the desire to signify, the students create poster-collages. Through pictures, fabrics, other surfaces, and objects, they try to signify the desire for (and the absence of) presence. Materials in former collages include cigarette papers, gum wrappers, colored chalk, postage stamps, heavily textured fabrics, soap bubble labels, stained woods, lipsticks of all shades and hues; printed phrases such as "You don't say so" and "You have my word on it"; pictures of barred windows, hills, prisoners, the sun, mouths of all sorts, and of course, tears and blank spaces. The effects of the collages when displayed are stunning; the walls writhe and shimmer with the materiality of absence and desire.

Section 2: A Script for A Feminist-Deconstructionist Staging

3/21/88

I don't understand my boyfriend is so completely disgusted by mine or any woman's menstrual cycle. We never even talk about "my period" we've substituted the word, Emily. (It's a long story) Anyway I always say "well Emily's here this week." How completely ridiculous isn't It?[13]

But from where does "Emily" come, if not our own classrooms, from the non-critical New Critical reading of poems such as Keats' "Bright

---

[13] Excerpts from a student's diary. The student mailed me a copy of these pages sometime in 1989, along with a letter to the effect that she had "come across" the diary and thought, since the entry pertained to our class, that I might like to have it.

Star," our willingness to republish and confess again the guilt of original sin?

> Bright star, would I were stedfast as thou art—
> Not in lone splendour hung aloft the night
> And watching, with eternal lids apart,
> Like nature's patient, sleepless Eremite,
> The moving waters at their priestlike task
> Of pure ablution round earth's human shores,
> Or gazing on the new soft-fallen mask
> Of snow upon the mountains and the moors—
> No—yet still stedfast, still unchangeable,
> Pillow'd upon my fair love's ripening breast,
> To feel for ever its soft fall and swell,
> Awake forever in a sweet unrest,
> Still, still to hear her tender-taken breath,
> And so live ever—or else swoon to death.

In a New Critical reading of Keats' sonnet, the purity of the star is guaranteed by its conceptual opposite: the *unclean* shores of earth. The world of the star is sexless, remote, spiritual, Platonic, constant, transcendent. The earth, by contrast, is subject to the work of time and human weakness: its shores are carnal, base, tarnished, and in need of "ablution."

From the sublunar world of the poem's sestet, what message gets flashed to adolescent women? For what must this earthly world receive "ablution" if not the stain of original sin, the "ripening" of the woman's body to sex? And to what erotic uses is the woman in the poem subjected? Stripped of language, denied a voice, she is fetishized as a "breast," written upon, and appropriated by the lover as a pillow.

The postmodern challenge is to stage a reading of Keats' sonnet that follows its textual contradictions, exposes its Platonism, shows its sexism, and opens onto student issues and concerns. The scenes below play on the differences between literal and figurative meanings of words and the discrepancy between what the lover *says* (he does not want to be like the star) and what he *does* (he devotes eight of the sonnet's fourteen lines to a consideration of the star).[14]

---

[14] In "Teaching Deconstructively," Barbara Johnson provides seven examples of textual conflicts a deconstructive reader might encounter: (1) Ambiguous words; (2) Undecidable

Mary Alice Delia

The Case of the Mad Swooner

A Feminist-Deconstructionist Reading of Keats' "Bright Star"

Scene One:	The Plunder of Fair Love
Characters:	Bright Star (played by a female in this version) I (played by a male in this version) Fair Love (played by a female in this version)
Props:	A pillow A glass of water (on floor) Cotton balls

As the scene opens, I and Fair Love are sitting on the floor, back-to-back.

Bright Star enters and takes a position facing I. Black mascara lines extend from her eyes outward in all directions, suggesting "eternal lids apart."

I: (Calls her by name) "Bright star! ... (Fair Love, thinking I has called her, turns and throws her arms lovingly around his neck. I throws her arms off and gazes admiringly at Bright Star.)

I: (Addressing Bright Star) "...would I were steadfast as thou art—" (Bright Star preens and dances happily; Fair Love glares angrily at I from the floor.)

I: "Not in lone splendor hung aloft the night / And watching, with eternal lids apart," (Bright Star tries to blink, frowns; tries to speak but no words come out. Fair Love passes her hand over I's eyes, trying to get his attention.)

I: "Like nature's patient, sleepless Eremite" (Bright Star doesn't like the comparison; she holds her nose up with her fingers. Fair Love waves her hands wildly in front of I's face.)

I: "The moving waters at their priest-like task / Of pure ablution round earth's human shores" (Fair Love throws drops of water at I's head, but I, entranced by Bright Star, shrugs the water off.)

---

syntax; (3) Incompatibilities between what a text says and what it does; (4) Incompatibilities between the literal and the figurative; (5) Incompatibilities between explicitly foregrounded assertions and illustrative examples or less explicitly asserted supporting material; (6) Obscurity; (7) Fictional self-interpretation (141-142) .

I: "Or gazing on the new soft-fallen mask" (Now Fair Love tickles I; laughing, he rolls on the floor.)

I: "Of snow upon the mountains and the moors— "(I can't stop laughing; Bright Star laughs, points at I, claps, and dances wordlessly.)

Alternative Ending A: {Rape}

I: "No—" (I grabs Fair Love and holds her arms down on the floor; Fair Love laughs.)

I: "—yet still steadfast, still unchangeable, / Pillowed upon my fair love's ripening breast, (I presses the pillow down on Fair Love's breast; Fair Love tries to get up.)

I: "To feel for ever its soft fall and swell, / Awake forever in a sweet unrest" (I puts his head on the pillow; Fair Love beats him with her fists.)

I: "Still, still to hear her tender-taken breath" / And so live ever— (I grabs Fair Love's hands with one hand, pins them to the floor.)

I: "or else...SWOON to death." (I puts the pillow over Fair Love's face; Fair Love screams wordlessly no no no no.)

Bright Star turns down the corners of her mouth, then turns around, facing the wall.

Alternative Ending B: {Murder}

I: "No- - "(I addresses Fair Love, grabs her, pins her arms to the floor, puts the pillow over her face and chest; Fair Love struggles to breathe.)

I: "—yet still steadfast, still unchangeable, / Pillowed upon my fair love's ripening breast, (I continues to address Fair Love who struggles to get up; I falls on the pillow to hold her down; Fair Love makes muffled sounds of protest.)

I: "To feel for ever its soft fall and swell, / Awake forever in a sweet unrest" (Fair Love's chest heaves violently; her arms flail.)

I: "Still, still to hear her tender-taken breath"/ And so live ever—" (Fair Love grabs I's hair and pulls wildly)

I: "or else... SWOON to death." (Fair Love slumps; her fingers fall from I's hair; she dies. Terrified, I stuffs the pillow under a chair and runs from the room.)

Bright Star turns down the corners of her mouth, then turns around, facing the wall.

13

Scene Two: "Bright Star's Revenge"

Characters & Props: I
                             Detective Columbo
                             Bright Star
                             Flashlight
                             Chair
                             Pillow
                             Toy Handcuffs

As the scene opens, Columbo is interrogating I. Bright Star is standing on the teacher's desk as we left her, with her back to the characters.

Columbo: Let's see if I've got this straight now. You arrived here at seven o'clock this morning and discovered Fair Love in the bedroom, dead. (Bright Star turns slowly around, yawns, stretches her arms)

I: That's right. Seven o'clock this morning, steadfast as always. I knocked; no one answered, so I let myself in. You can't imagine my ... shock to find my Fair Love dead. (Bright Star jumps up and down trying to get Columbo's attention; she tries to speak, but no words come from her mouth.)

Columbo: Yeah, well, I dunno. There's something here I just can't put my finger on. (Columbo looks around the room.) I keep telling myself, it just ain't natural. A young pretty girl like that, to swoon to death.

I: I don't understand it myself. Last night, things were just fine. (I kneels over Fair Love's body.) If you don't mind, Lieutenant, I'd like to take a last picture of her. (I takes a close-up shot of Fair Love's breast; Columbo regards him in amazement; Bright Star, frantic, begins to look in the drawers of the teacher's desk for something, anything.)

Columbo: I dunno. Something about this just doesn't seem right to me. If only there were a witness or a murder weapon. (Columbo looks up at Bright Star.) Say, do you see that star? Must be the morning star. Mrs. Columbo? She knows all about the stars. I'll have to ask her about this. (Bright Star finds a flashlight, shakes it, tries to figure out what it is.)

I: If that's all, lieutenant, may I go? Being here with her, you know... (I takes a tissue from the teacher's desk, dabs at his eyes. Bright Star accidentally turns the flashlight on. She jumps in fright, peers into it, then smiles and shines it directly on the pillow stuffed under the chair.)

Columbo: Say, what's going on here? What's making all that light? I believe, sir, that star is shining right in here in this very room.

I: Star? What star? I don't see any star.

Columbo: (Columbo points to Bright Star). Yes, sir, would you look at that? Now that's one bright star. I'll sure have to tell Mrs. Columbo about this one. Here it's (Columbo checks his watch) 7:10 in the morning and would you just look how bright that star is!

(Bright Star preens; (I starts to tip toe toward the door. Columbo follows the light to the pillow stuffed under the chair)

Columbo: Well, well, what's this? A pillow! Now would you look at this, sir!

I: What's that? I never saw that pillow before! Someone must have put it there!

Columbo: Say, you don't see very good, do you? Know what I think, sir? This lady here, she didn't swoon. This pillow right here, has hair on it. Sir, do you know what I think? This lady has been *swooned*.

(I turns and runs out the door. Columbo slowly takes out a pair of handcuffs, walks leisurely to the door, then turns and addresses Bright Star) Well, what do you know? Finally, I got to see the morning star.

(Columbo scratches his head and addresses the class.) Say, isn't there a poem about that somewhere? Star... light... star... bright star, would I were... nope, it just don't come to me. I'll just have to ask Mrs. Columbo. Stars! that's *her* department. (Exits)

Section 3: Deconstructing *Hamlet*

Alice was beginning to get very tired of sitting by her sister on the bank, and of having nothing to do; once or twice she had peeped into the book her sister was reading, but it had no pictures or conversations in it, 'and what is the use of a book', thought Alice, 'without pictures or conversations'?

— Lewis Carroll, *The Annotated Alice*, 25

Hamlet

Setting: Graduate Seminar on Theory/Pedagogy

Characters: Figgy (Teacher)
                                 Notetaker (Student)
                                 Globekeeper (Student)
                                 Other Players (Students)

Props & Materials:
Academic robe (see *Academic Robe*, Chapter 5)
Bell (old-fashioned, with long handle)
Globe (small, spinning).[15]
Slate (3" × 5") with chalk and eraser (see Slate, Chapter 5)
Noise makers (New Year's Eve horns or twirlers to announce the deconstructive operation as a celebration)
Hamlet (Covered and retitled HAMLET: THE TRUE TEXT)
Hamlet Packets (shown in the lesson)

Opening Scene:

Figgy enters the classroom dressed in an academic robe accented by several long strands of pink pearls and/or rhinestones, tooting and twirling noise-makers.[16] She takes *HAMLET: THE TRUE TEXT* from her bookbag and displays its title. She gives **Globekeeper** the globe with instructions to keep a finger on Denmark throughout the class period. She gives **Notetaker** the 3" x 5" slate with instructions to take "lots and lots" of notes.

Old notes can be erased to make room for new notes. **Figgy** then distributes the *Hamlet* packets to the students.

---

[15] The globe is a useful prop for dramatizing Derrida's idea that "the game is the play of the world" and that "He who tipped the axis of the globe could have been a player God, unknowingly risking the best and the worst at the same time" (*OG* 259-260).

[16] **Figgy** can also start the scene by randomly throwing objects about the room: playing cards, dice, jumping jacks, chess pieces, or any object or apparatus that suggests risk, chance, gambling. Another "scene start" requires three simultaneous operations. As backdrop, construct the word *HAMLET* from alphabet blocks. The scene requires three student volunteers. At the blow of a horn (or a wave of a baton), one student will tip over the "h" in the word *hamlet*; another will wind and play a musical clown; another will spin a small globe on its axis. Give several students the alphabet blocks and ask them to occupy themselves during the lesson by forming as many words from the HAMLET letters as possible.

Figgy: Good morning, students. Today we will analyze the meaning of Shakespeare's great drama, *Hamlet*. We will begin by looking at three elements of its structure: character, plot, and language. First, however, I want us to feel confident that *TRUE TEXT* (holds up *Hamlet*: ...) is the one-and-only, definitive version of Shakespeare's play. To confirm its status, I will review *Hamlet's* textual history. **Notetaker**, get ready to go. My lecture contains 333 words and takes approximately one minute to deliver.

Figgy's Lecture: The Textual History of *Hamlet*[17]

The earliest known copy of the first quarto of *Hamlet* was first thought an imperfect reproduction of an earlier version of the *Hamlet* of the second quarto which claims on its title page to be "enlarged to almost as much again as it was, according to the true and perfect Coppie" (Craig 898). Later the first quarto of *Hamlet* was thought a "badly botched version of the true text" which was taken down during a performance of *Hamlet* by a pirate and either that person or "an indifferent poet" revised this version of *Hamlet* for the press (899). Meanwhile, there is evidence to show that these same passages in *Hamlet* may have been pirated by the actor who earlier had given corrupted quartos to the printer; there is also evidence to show that Hamlet was written twice; the first quarto, therefore, would be a corruption of a first draft; it is possible that all the parts of the first quarto of *Hamlet* not corresponding to the second quarto were made up by actors but all this has nothing to do with the theory of how the first quarto of *Hamlet* came into being; there are definite, certifiable traces in *Hamlet* of an early revenge play called *Hamlet*; the earlier *Hamlet*, alluded to by Thomas Nashe in 1589, was probably ground out "like a hack writer by candlelight": also, prior to 1600, a play called *Hamlet* was acted in Germany and this version of *Hamlet* was modernized and preserved *as Fratricide Punished* in 1710; like the old *Hamlet* written by the hack, this *Hamlet* had a ghost demanding revenge, a secret murder and adultery, feigned madness, the play-within-the-play, the sparing of the king, the voyage to England, Ophelia's madness, and poisoned foils; also a *Hamlet*-saga is alluded to in Scandinavian literature as early as the tenth century (898-900) A *Hamlet* is also a village, a little grouping of houses in the country, as well as a food fish found from Florida to the southern West Indies. (Rings BELL) THE END!

Figgy: Notetaker, I hope you got all that down. Remember, as a student, your job is to preserve and re-publish what I say. (Looks askance at the notetaker's slate) Is this your idea of a joke? Or a sign of a mental breakdown? Hereafter, you must try to do better."

---

[17] Materials extracted from Craig 898.

"All right, class, now that you have heard *Hamlet's* convoluted textual history, you can understand why I have gone to such lengths to make sure that our text is the one, *true* text. Well? (displays *True Text*), What do you think? Is it or is it not the true text of *Hamlet*?

"What do you mean, you 'aren't sure'? Were you *listening*? Is there something wrong with your *ears*?"

"I hope you read better than you listen. We will now look at three of the play's characters: Hamlet, Ophelia, and Laertes. Turn to Page 1 of your *Hamlet* packets and read Claudius's descriptions of these characters. Then, follow the instructions as the bottom of the page. As you know, I am one of the few members of the department willing to try a new idea in the classroom, providing, that is, that it takes no more than five minutes of class time. You have five minutes. Begin reading *now*.

Claudius:

.... 0 Gertrude, Gertrude,
When sorrows come, they come not single spies,
But in battalions. First, her father slain;
Next, *your son gone*; and he most violent author
Of his own just remove; the people muddied,
Thick and unwholesome in their thoughts and whispers,
For good Polonius' death, and we have done but greenly,
In hugger- mugger to inter him; poor Ophelia
Divided from herself and her fair judgement,
Without the which we are pictures or mere beasts;
Last, and as much containing as all these,
Her brother is in secret come from France;
Feeds on his wonder, keeps *himself in clouds*,
And wants not buzzers to infect his ear
With pestilent speeches of his father's death,
Wherein necessity, of matter beggar'd,
Will nothing stick our person to arraign
In ear and ear... (IV. v. 77-94. Emphasis mine)

Three-Minute Activity: On the back of this page or on your own paper, draw pictures of:[18]

1. Hamlet ("a son gone")
2. Ophelia ("divided from herself")
3. Laertes ("himself in clouds")

Figgy: (At the end of five minutes, ringing the bell loudly) Stop! Stop! Stop immediately! All right, let's see your character depictions (looks at the drawings and scowls). You call those *character* portrayals? Where are the characters? Where's Laertes? Where's Ophelia? Where's Hamlet? You're supposed to be drawing characters here, not clouds!

I will give you one more chance. Horatio speaks of Hamlet. Perhaps you will find his words more helpful than Claudius's. Turn to Page 2 of your packets and read Horatio's speech.

Page 2
(Picture of bodies of five brutally mutilated soldiers)

Picture Caption

"Now cracks a noble heart. Good night, sweet prince,
And flights of angels sing thee to thy rest!"

Figgy: (glowering at the handout) "Oh, no! Another Greensplatt Screw-up! Greensplatt works part-time for the English department and part-time for history and he's forever getting the two mixed up. At this point, we will forego the analysis of character and go directly to the analysis of the play's language. We will look first at Hamlet's soliloquy, "To be or not to be," on Page 3 of your packet. Susie Q, will you volunteer to read it aloud?

---

[18] Large crayons, if available, can be given to students who want them.

Mary Alice Delia

THE SUICIDE
Joyce Carol Oates

didn't acknowledge receipt
didn't wave goodbye
didn't flutter the air with kisses a mound of tinsel gifts
unwrapped
air mail letters unopened
bedclothes rumpled
No thank you

always elsewhere

though it was raining elsewhere
though strange-speaking persons people the streets
the minarets might have been dangerous
the drinking water suspect
though we at home slaved and baked
and wept and dialed the phone
and hung tinsel ornaments
did he marvel
did he thank
was he grateful   did he know
was he considerate
was he human
was he there

To be, or not to be, that is the question:
Whether 'tis nobler in the mind to suffer
The slings and arrows of outrageous fortune
Or to take arms against a sea of troubles,
And by opposing end them.

Always elsewhere!
didn't thank
didn't kiss
toothbrush stiffened
cat scratching at the screen
car battery dead

was that human?

Went where?

Figgy: (enraged) Not again! How in the world did that other text get into this text, I mean our text, Hamlet's soliloquy, *True Text, Hamlet's speech?*

Well, there's no helping it. At least we still have the plot, the one remaining element of the play's structure. To show you how an analysis of the plot can reveal the play's meaning, I've solicited the help of two professional plot investigators, Monsieur Poirot and Ltd. Columbo. Please show your appreciation by smiling and clapping your hands.

The Case of *Hamlet*
Featuring Poirot and Columbo

P.	It wears a beard
C.	But the length is "indeterminable"
P.	It looks like ...
C	.... but is not the King
P.	It is a ghost,
C.	but is it the King's ghost?
P.	It appears ...
C.	... and disappears
P.	It walks on the ground ...
C.	... but speaks from under it
P.	I saw him yesterday, or t'other day
C.	Or then, or then, with such, or such,
P.	Words we don't know the meaning of ...
C.	... like "eale"
P,	Madness ...
C.	... the presence or absence of
P.	An audience watching Hamlet ...
C.	... watching a King
P.	... watching a play
C.	A play that precedes the possibility for action
P.	Ophelia who grieves she has seen what she has seen
C.	Sees what she sees but doesn't see at all
P.	Rosencrantz and Gildenstern deny they were sent for
C.	But appear, then disappear
P.	Questions of reliability
C.	A text inscribed on the "table" of Hamlet's "memory"
P.	Within the "book and volume of his brain"
C.	A prior text, a pre-text
P.	"The Murder of Ganzago"
C.	His own writing, an invention
P.	Ruptures, fissures, puns
C.	Graves without bodies

P.   Skulls without graves
C.   Horatio, who promises Hamlet never to tell
P.   Then promises Hamlet to tell all
C.   Mistaken identities
P.   Lies, outright lies
C.   What to make of it?
P.   Uncertainties
C.   Accidental judgments
P.   Casual slaughters
C.   Plots and errors
P.   Hmmmm ...
C.   What can it mean?
P.   My dear chap, I am sure I don't know.

(Columbo and Poirot exit)

Figgy: "So, what does the plot tell us about the play's meaning? What do you mean you 'can't follow' it? It's a pretty straightforward account if you ask me. I don't understand what's wrong with you people. I gave you the complete rundown on *Hamlet's* textual history and in return, you gave me the runaround on the question of *The True Text*. I asked you to draw three characters from the play as Claudius describes them. In turn, you gave me pictures with no people in them.

"Now you say you can't make sense of the plot. Poirot and Columbo do their job; the problem is, you don't do yours. You don't listen; you can't draw, and it's clear from your failure to find one theme of the play in Hamlet's soliloquy that you can't even *read!*

"I must say that never in my long career, have I ever been given a class as incompetent as this one. I'll tell you straight out that every student in this room is in danger of failing the course. **Globekeeper** and **Notetaker** have already flunked and may as well withdraw. **Globekeeper** did not keep a finger on Denmark as instructed; she amused herself by spinning the globe. **Notetaker** spent more time erasing my words than writing them down.

"Very well. The assignment for next week is to write a fifty-page analysis of the characters, plot, theme, setting, mood, symbolism, imagery and whatever else you can think of, in *Hamlet*.

Angrily, Figgy packs up. She pitches *HAMLET: THE TRUE TEXT* into her book bag, stalks to the door, stops, turns, blows a noisemaker, and snaps: "Make that fifty-five"!
End of Lesson

Section 4: The Seminar Critiques

What Worked

Student 1: ... hilarious, troubling, powerful, quirky, fun ... I appreciate play so much more than the 'nihilistic' results of postmodern theory ... I liked the pictures ... That intertextual factor works. I cannot, as teacher or student, ever approach *Hamlet* again with pat answers to its complexities ... I loved the juxtaposition of the Joyce Carol Oates poem with Hamlet's soliloquy. And the drawing exercise!! Opl/2helia divided from herself—an apt metaphor for deconstruction.

Student 2: That was fun! There it was, the great *Hamlet* disseminated in hundreds of other texts; its authority as 'the' text undermined by pre-texts and post-texts claiming to be recognized as constituent parts of 'the' text (I think that the idea of deconstructing also the authority figure of the teacher - who is the one who helps to stress the authority of 'the' text - played a fundamental role). It was a liberation for me ... I hate *Hamlet*, mainly because I hate Hamlet—that self-centered little monster - yet, I still have reverence for it and I still feel that there must be some profound meaning hidden in it which I'll never be able to grasp. Well, I was happy to see it demystified by the interaction of other texts, including my drawings .... And I believe that undergraduates would have felt the same feeling of release since I'm sure they share many of my fears.

Student 3: You might have explained deconstruction for a hundred years but you'd have never evoked the feel of it as you did in those twenty minutes or so. My favorite parts: when you let me have the blackboard to take notes on which would then be erased .... Questions about the viability and power of language were all condensed in your visual, palpable metaphor of the tiny blackboard. My erasing it was a gesture of futility such as I've rarely experienced...

Student 4: What was most impressive for me was the very first exercise we did: identification of all the versions of the play as the 'Hamlet' we all know and love ... Perhaps by showing that *Hamlet* is many stories, the instructor can de-mystify the play that we do end up working with and encourage students not to fear what is in front of them.

As the students' comments confirm, the deconstructionist operation is not a treasure hunt for truth, at least not in the traditional sense of uncovering or discovering a truth-object. Instead, it tries, through graftings, parody, puns, and other textual plays, to multiply "the outside in itself," to increase the play of representation. The setting for the *Hamlet* lesson is "the hall of the theatre," or a classroom that makes use of "the games and detours of representation" (*OG* 307).

Six of the lesson's "games and detours" are identified by the seminar students as especially effective: the juxtapositioning of texts (Oates' poem, graphic war pictures); the play of dissemination (*Hamlet's* textual history); the attack on teacher-authority (Figgy's screw-ups); the use of hands-on objects and props (bell, noisemakers, globe, slate); the inclusion of student-generated materials (drawings); the critique of imitation (the slate). If, as Ulmer believes, the "central problem for postructural education is how to deconstruct the function of imitation in the pedagogic effect" (AG 174), what could be more hostile to imitation than the taking and erasing of notes on a 3×5-inch chalkboard?

Nearly all the critiques approved the attack on the teacher as site-of-authority. The importance of challenging professorial power is stressed in theory/pedagogy literature but with few consequences (as yet) for actual classrooms. Many articles assume that the teacher-authority problem is solved by adopting a culturally inclusive curriculum. A few articles offer single stroke solutions: they attempt to lose the teacher in a circle or squirrel her away in a desk at the back of the room. One essay (since I cannot now locate it, readers will simply have to take my word for it), recommends that the teacher remove herself by sitting on the floor in a remote corner of the room.[19]

The problem of deconstructing teacher authority[20] is a tough one for pedagogy and I make no claim to solve it here. However, one point of the *Hamlet* lesson is that a teacher intent on deconstructing the traditional classroom cannot separate her own practice from its institutional structures. As Derrida writes, the "movements of deconstruction do not destroy structures from the outside": they attack from within, "by inhabiting" them "*in a certain way*" (*OG* 24). Strategies for inhabiting the classroom are addressed in the final section of this chapter, following a presentation of the concerns expressed by the graduate students in their critiques.

---

[19] There is nothing silly about sitting on the floor if the positioning is self-reflexive, e.g., a text-worshipper showing herself by *kneeling* on the floor.

[20] [*Ed.*] For a recent perspective on this issue, please check Yusofi, M., Zarghami-Hamrah, S., Ghaedy, Y., & Mahmudnia, A. (2017). Deconstruction as an approach for removing hierarchical teacher–student relations. *Policy Futures in Education, 16*, 147821031773620. The authors reject the binary oppositiuon between teacher and students, and highlight that students should assume a more active role in the educational process, dealing with the discovery and construction of knowledge in an action-based process.

Questions & Concerns

While the seminar students enjoyed the performative aspects of the lesson—its gleeful (and spiteful) spirit, funky, theatrical moves, outrageous self-posturing—they also express concerns about the appropriateness of deconstruction theory for what one graduate student calls "the naive freshman college student." Because others in the academic community share the seminar students' anxieties, I reproduce their comments here.[21]

Student 1: Do the students benefit? Can they enjoy your deconstruction in the same way that we as ENGL 758 students do-by seeing an application of the theory in concrete terms? Can your students work within the traditional mode of New Criticism first and then move towards the more demanding postmodern stuff? I may sound nervous and conventional here, but the questions arise from a concern for the receivers, the maturing reader, the naive freshman college student. What is Hamlet, then, after deconstruction?

Student 2: Where do we go from here? . . . Should I go ahead and deconstruct this meaning as well? Do I want to do that? When does my—and your other students'— moment of construction (affirmation) come? Never? Only for a brief 'strategic' moment which must be deconstructed immediately after? That's scary!

Student 3: While I loved the presentation for us, I could not imagine doing the whole thing or most of it for high school or early college students. The reason it works so beautifully for us ... is that we understand the conventions of language and literature you were disrupting. It seems that an understanding of the conventional structures and attitudes must be in place before you can deconstruct or subvert.

I could see teaching students *Hamlet* in some more traditional way—whether New Critical, Feminist, Archetypal or whatever and then on the last day of the unit make them question what you have just done with a deconstructive exercise or two; but, I cannot see doing only deconstruction when they don't know what they are deconstructing.

Student 4: Once the slippery slope of deconstruction begins its slide, what would prevent one from deconstructing the added texts and presumably, the new text which arose from the joining of the two, previously isolated texts, etc., etc., etc.

---

[21] The excerpts in this section are not taken, necessarily, from the same critiques shown earlier, i.e., "Student 1" in this section is not the "Student 1" in this section.

Two important issues surface in these responses; one has to do with practical considerations and the other, with ethics. The graduate students want to know how, realistically, undergraduates can be expected to deconstruct a text they do not yet apprehend as a construct. The students also worry about deconstruction's so-called "nihilistic" effects on the undergraduate psyche. As a student (not quoted above) observed: "Isn't the teacher obligated to help students achieve meaning, not pull the epistemological rug out from under their feet?"

In response to the latter, deconstruction does not kill off meaning. A practice driven by deconstruction theory does not arrive at the morgue. The very mark and sign of a postmodern classroom is its refusal to submit, its resistance to the final sealing of the eyes.[22] Granted, a deconstructionist classroom is uncertain but within the practice of uncertainty are techniques for helping undergraduates defend against closure and the discourses of meaning. In the face of the other's perspective, the undergraduate is powerless. She has no techniques for interrogating (defending against) the discourse of meaning, no theoretical base from which to challenge, for example, the vocabularies of thematic criticism prevalent in most English classrooms.

At "seventeen something," students, like all of us, inhabit a world defined by conceptual oppositions; students, however, have few strategies for keeping open the space between conceptual oppositions, for finding a way to "inhabit" or interrogate truth statements and either-or propositions. What deconstruction offers are strategies for unweaving some of these oppositions, techniques for undoing the false dichotomies which the media transmits and which the traditional classroom, knowingly or not, supports. Students can learn from deconstruction, for example, how to use one of its most powerful tools for opening language, the *chiasmus*, to challenge the scene of pedagogy itself: do we teach what is true? Or are things true because we teach them?

"Deconstruction, I have insisted," Derrida writes in a letter to Jean-Louis Houdebine, is "not *neutral*. It *intervenes*" (*Positions* 93). Deconstruction's interventions, moreover, are arguably the most sophisticated, linguistically nuanced tools available to the contemporary classroom. Drawing from a seemingly inexhaustible repertoire of

---

[22] To show that idea, use a doll with open-and-close eyes. Enact its death by closing its eyes and covering its face with a blanket.

linguistic operations-chiasma, ellipsis, pun, pivot, lateral association, literal meaning, dissemination, fold, homonym, graft—deconstruction liberates and frees the word to play. Students will not learn from deconstruction how best to live, but they can learn how, by keeping the word alive, to keep alive and extend their options ("An Interview with Derrida" 81).

To imagine deconstruction's power to extend options and sustain life *literally*, recall the dialogue leading up to the final scene between Neal Perry and his father in the film *Dead Poets Society*. Neal is afraid to tell his father that he wants to become an actor, not a doctor. "My father is making me quit the play," Neal tells his teacher, Keating, approaching him in the privacy of his quarters. "He's planning the rest of my life for me and he's never asked me what I want."

"You have to talk to him," Keating said.

"I can't," Neal replied. "I can't talk to him."

"You have to talk to him before tomorrow night," Keating urged.

"Prove your passion for acting by your conviction."

"I can't talk to him," Neal repeated. "I'm trapped."

"No, you're not!" Keating challenged, but the very next

night, Neal put a gun to his head.

Rather than giving Neal tools to deconstruct his father's logic, Keating gives him a pep talk. It simply is "not true" that Neal cannot talk to his father. Neal *can*. All he needs to "seize the day" is the power of his passion and conviction! In Keating's epistemology, "passion" and "conviction" constitute solid evidence, solid ways of knowing; to Neal's father, however, it is "discipline" and "self-denial" that signify, not the "absurd business of acting." Trapped between two polarized perspectives, Neal is powerless. "You *will* go to medical school," his father tells him. "You *will* become a doctor."

"But—but I've got to tell you how *I* feel," Neal protests.

"Well, go ahead," his father snaps. "Tell me."

Impatiently, he waits for Neal to speak. But silence is Neal's only reply.

Silence *need* not have been Neal's only reply. Had he known how to attack the logic of his father's binary thinking, he might have argued:

"Look, Dad, I don't get this 'you *will* become a doctor' stuff. I mean, you have to agree there's a possibility I won't. Even if I wanted to, I might not make it. Lots of people don't, you know. I might get AIDS or I might crack up. I don't plan to, but those things do happen to people and they could happen to me.

Or, "Dad, you seem to think the operating room and the theatre are opposite ends of some kind of pole, but is that the case? Both doctors and actors are performers. Isn't a medical operation something like a theatre performance? Both have an audience, costumes, props, lights. Isn't there a point, in fact, where the difference between being a doctor and being an actor isn't all that great?"

This is still not to respond to the seminar student's question of how students can be expected to deconstruct what has not yet been constructed, or how deconstruction can inhabit structure in a classroom when structure itself is not yet in place. The answer, for many teachers, is that it cannot. Those same teachers, however, would likely agree there is something inherently unfair in teaching students to construct readings that at some later point in time, they may be asked to deconstruct. The solution, perhaps, is to acknowledge that we are now in a new and challenging pedagogical situation, one requiring us to teach students how to close and open the text *at the same time*, as zippers annoyingly do sometimes, on coats and suitcases.

Figgy's operations in the *Hamlet* demonstration lesson are too thick-and-fast for students barely conversant with formalist structures, but her deconstruct-as-you-go approach does address certain pedagogical problems. Rather than build and then blow-up castles (operations each requiring long periods of instructional time) the teacher can, in one session, construct and then deconstruct a castle-building tool, the structuralist use of plot analysis to construct meaning, for example, or any device used in a traditional classroom to construct literary edifices.

Although the *Hamlet* lesson has methodological implications for the deconstruction classroom, its operations are not intended as routines. There are as many ways to inhabit traditional structures as there are differences, at any given moment, among and within classrooms. Those who fear deconstruction will become formulaic, think primarily of its operations on the literary text, not the interplay of its text with the text of the classroom. The difference of a postmodern pedagogy is, in part, the difference of the *classroom*: the differences constituted by race, class, gender, age; the diversity of values, intellectual assumptions, cultural and ethnic backgrounds, individual interests, career and life goals, learning styles, prior academic experiences.

"Derrida does not have a pedagogy," Ulmer writes, but "he encourages others to imagine (and then enact) what a deconstructive teaching might be like" (AP 158). Although there is no consensus (nor should there be) on what a deconstructive pedagogy might look like, we would agree, I think, that it cannot "take place" in a room with no giggles, no mask or wink, no sign or mark of the disruption of presence. At the very least, from a theory as performance conscious and playfully parodic as deconstruction, the classroom deserves more than "English as usual." Ingenious, tricky, spaced-out, a deconstructist pedagogy has as many moves up its sleeve as writing itself has for multiplying the *outside*: pantomime, parody, dance, mask, exchange, to suggest only a few.

Although deconstruction's techniques for deferring meaning are not invulnerable and although in time, the "difference" of deconstruction theory may be displaced by theories more open to issues that are current and political, it offers much to a pedagogy that knows how to use its tools in the interests of students. A deconstructionist pedagogy, moreover, is not grim and depressing, but celebratory. It does not focus on the "sad, *negative*" side of deconstruction, but on what Derrida calls the "other side" of the coin, the joy of a world "offered to an active interpretation" (*Structure, Sign, and Play* 264).

Mary Alice Delia

CHAPTER TWO
Projects for A Deconstructionist Practice

Plato often uses the example of letters of the alphabet in order to come to grips with a problem. They give him a better grip on things; that is, he can use them to explain dialectics-but he never 'comes to grips with' the writing he uses.

— Derrida, *Dissemination,* 159

Most readers would agree that a classroom which takes as its first question, the question of what writing *is* (*OG* 74), should help students acquire knowledge of the alphabet. Interrogating grammatology or writing as "a positive science," Derrida asks: "What is writing?" "How can it be identified?" "Where and when does one pass from one writing to another, from writing in general to writing in the narrow sense…?" (*OG* 74-75). Derrida's questions pose a formidable challenge to the classroom, one made more problematic by deconstruction's hostility to programmatic instruction. The strategy of this chapter is to follow Derrida's method in *Of Grammatology*, of moving from the inquiry into literal, graphic, inscription as writing, to the interrogation of writing as "all that gives rise to inscription in general, whether it is literal or not… "(*OG* 9).

Derrida's pedagogy is seen in this chapter's two sections or "stages'' of inquiry. The first section focuses on the play of writing in the alphabet; the second, on the play of writing beyond the alphabet. The activities in the first section are intended to increase students' understanding of language operations and to provide opportunities for tinkering[1] and experimenting. The activities in the second section are designed to help

---

[1] [*Ed.*] Tinkering is a pedagogical method and an experiential approach to learning based on the exploration, creation, and construction of knowledge about the world. It has become very popular in recent years and it has been widely adopted in formal and informal learning settings. Its combination with new technologies has led to the development of some applications to support the implementation of Tinkering in several leaning contexts at various levels; for example, the Let's Tinker App is widely used for Tinkering in the context of STEM education. Recent research has highlighted that Tinkering could be adopted not only to develop students' knowledge but also to support thinking processes, such as critical thinking and creative problem solving, thus switching from Tinkering to Thinkering (e.g., Poce, A., Amenduni, F., & De Medio, C. (2019). From Tinkering to Thinkering: Tinkering as Critical and Creative Thinking Enhancer. *Journal of E-Learning and Knowledge Society, 15*(2), 101-112).

students understand the idea of writing as anything distributed in space (things "pictorial, musical, sculptural") and provide opportunities for students to practice writing beyond the alphabet (*OG* 9).

The above overview would seem to imply a series of ready-to-use handouts, programmed to move students from Point A to B. Assuredly, that is not the case. The chapter is a loosely knit gathering of "things tried in the classroom," a potpourri of anecdotal narratives, project descriptions and assignments, transcripts of teacher-student exchanges, scripts prepared in advance of class and scripts generated on site. The activities and projects described in this chapter are meant to work with or without the "literary" text; in or out of conjunction with readings from Derrida.[2] Readers themselves will know when and how best to introduce or weave (or not, depending) the chapter's ideas into their own lesson plans.

Section 1: Writing with the Alphabet

In most English classrooms, students work, rather than play, with language. They expect to receive, and are given, techniques and strategies for structuring themes or thesis papers. This sort of writing Derrida calls "Platonic," writing that tries to conceal, rather than open to play, the multiple meanings of words. What Platonic writing tries to exclude—the play of all possible meanings of a word, including those lurking in its synonyms, homonyms—Derrida seeks to include. For Derrida, the word is a link in a "chain of significations" that as Derrida demonstrates in his own writing, has no closure, no end (*Diss* 129). The play of meaning, the word's tireless and irksome ability to translate and mean differently, is precisely what a traditional classroom tries to close off and what a deconstructionist classroom struggles to keep open.

The activities and projects described in this section enable students to experience, *through* play, the play of signification. The first activity helps give students an understanding of closure or of how, traditionally, the play of signification is stopped. This activity is followed by exercises that probe the ability of language to play at three levels: letter, word, and sentence. The section ends with an experimental writing project based on

---

[2] I concur with those who recommend reading *Of Grarrnnatology* as an introduction to deconstruction theory, for students as well as teachers. As conceptual support for the activities in this chapter, students might also read "Plato's Pharmacy," the longest (but most accessible) section of *Dissemination* and Roland Barthes' *The Pleasure of the Text*, a text rich in ideas for language play.

Raymond Federman's call for a self-reflexive fiction. While some of the activities intend no more than to exercise linguistic facility and quicken the spirit of play, others, like the writing project, require a more substantial time commitment.

SAC: Students Against Closure

Before learning strategies for keeping meaning open, students need to recognize and "come to grips with" the techniques of closure, the attempt, through language, to ground meaning in a Megabook, a doctrine, precept, credo, or set of beliefs that dictates the meaning of language and "puts a lid on" its play.

To show the presence of the Megabook in the classroom, display the *Bible* and Plato's *Republic*; give each student a section of grounding wire and the text of a poem, e.g., Keats' sonnet, "Bright Star." Explain that the idea is to discuss the poem's "meaning" without recourse to the wire, without "grounding" interpretation in dogma, e.g., the *Bible* or the *Republic*.[3] Determinations and judgments can be made by students representing SAC, or Students Against Closure. The panel is responsible for taking students who use the wire out of play and for recognizing (perhaps certificating) students who discuss the meaning of Keats' poem without recourse to a "higher authority" or "gospel truth."

What would seem to be a straightforward exercise is, for most students, an exercise in frustration. The students' attempts to defer meaning are met at every level by the natural desire to find meaning and foreclose on it, or in the language of cinema, to do a "Take!" on the reading rather than reshoot it. "Takes" of the sonnet's octave typically appeal to the platonic concept of transcendence, to a world that unlike our own, is timeless, unchanging, remote, chaste, sexless. Other "Takes" appeal to the Biblical notion of a world divided, from the beginning, between good and evil, sacred and profane.[4] On the "sacred side" of the opposition are images, words, and phrases (language) grounded in the

---

[3] See the discussion of "Grounding Wire" in Chapter 5 (listed alphabetically in postmodern props).

[4] The question "If the world didn't *come* divided, who divides it"? provokes excellent discussion. To set a stage for the discussion of binary oppositional thinking, give each student a small twig or piece of chalk and ask them to draw a line in the "sand" or on the "sidewalk." Then ask each student to explain what part of the world he or she is "dividing." The students love this activity; they remember the line-in-the-sand scene from childhood.

Biblical concepts of purity and redemption; on the "profane side" are images, words, and phrases grounded in the Biblical concepts of impurity, carnal knowledge, and sin. On the "positive" side, students *can* and *do* learn how to avoid closure—when taught skills for opening language and given the opportunity to practice.

At Play with the Letter

> *I will speak, therefore, of a letter.*
> *Of the first letter, if the alphabet, and most of the*
> *speculations which have ventured into it, are to be believed.*
> *I will speak, therefore, of the letter **a**, ...*

— Derrida, *Différance, 3*

> *This rag of scarlet cloth, - for time and wear and a*
> *sacrilegious moth had reduced it to little other than a*
> *rag, - on careful examination, assumed the shape of a*
> *letter. It was the capital letter A.*

— Nathaniel Hawthorne, *The Scarlet Letter*

Where the h_ is

No text for focusing the eye on the letter is more effective than Catherine M. Fanshawe's poem, "The Riddle." Ask the students to group themselves in teams, distribute the poem, and announce that the first group to solve the puzzle wins won dollar bill. (To experience the students' experience, try solving the puzzle yourself, before looking at the footnote).

The Riddle
— Catherine M. Fanshawe

'Twas whispered in Heaven, 'twas muttered in hell,
And echo caught faintly the sound as it fell;
On the confines of earth 'twas permitted to rest,
And the depths of the ocean its presence confess'd;
'Twill be found in the sphere when 'tis riven asunder,
Be seen in the lightning and heard in the thunder;
'Twas allotted to man with his earliest breath,
Attends him at birth and awaits him at death,

Presides o'er his happiness, honor, and health,
Is the prop of his house, and the end of his wealth.
In the heaps of the miser 'tis hoarded with care,
But is sure to be lost on his prodigal heir;
It begins every hope, every wish it must bound,
With the husbandman toils, and with monarchs is crowned;
Without it the seaman and soldier may roam,
But woe to the wretch who expels it from home!
In the whispers of conscience its voice will be found,
Nor e'er in the whirlwind of passion be drowned;
'Twill soften the heart; but though deaf be the ear,
It will make him acutely and instantly hear.
Set in shade, let it rest like a delicate flower;
Ah! breathe on it softly, it dies in an hour.[5]

When the puzzle is solved and the winning group clamors for its prize, write the words "won dollar bill" on the board. Tell the students the dollar bill is not available; it has already been "won." As a follow-up, invite students to write their own letter riddles.

At Play with the Word

> 'When we were little,' the Mock Turtle went on at
> last, more calmly, though still sobbing a little now and
> then, 'we went to school in the sea. The master was an
> old Turtle—we used to call him Tortoise—'
> 'Why did you call him Tortoise, if he wasn't one?' Alice asked.
> 'We called him Tortoise because he taught us,' said the
> Mock Turtle angrily. 'Really you are very dull!'

— Alice in Wonderland, 127

Into the Abyss!

The activity described below accomplishes in about twenty minutes what in most classrooms, would require much more time. The goal is to help students understand Derrida's idea that the meaning of a word is not fixed but open always to translation; how, through the play of puns, word

---

[5] The letter *H.*

associations, graftings and other language maneuvers, the meaning of a word is "kept alive."

The activity itself is quite simple: it requires students to brainstorm words or phrases containing or associated with a single word, e.g., the color *green*. As a technique for generating writing ideas, brainstorming has become a pedagogical staple; what is new (and memorable) about *this* activity is its "triple axel," the play of three back-to-back sessions rather than one. Whereas a typical brainstorming session has a single burst of ideas lasting five or ten minutes, this session has three distinct "bursts" or levels, one after the other, marked by intervening pauses or "dry spells." The third "burst" is marked by intense cognitive activity; word associations are prone to be richer, more provocative, more an effect of Derrida's own techniques for moving a word from one context to another.

On the day of the exercise, the students arrived in class to find on the board, the words: "Green, green, I want you green."

"What you are looking at," I told the class, "is the first line of "Somnambulistic Ballad," a poem by Federico Garcia Lorca. Lorca was a revolutionary. Imagine we, too, are revolutionaries and are, at this very moment, facing a firing squad. For some insane reason—a captor's caprice or sick sense of humor—we can escape death for exactly as long as we can keep the meaning of Lorca's poem, beginning with the meaning of the word green, alive and open to play. I will begin. Green, green, the jolly green giant!"[6]

> Fried green tomatoes!
> Green eggs and ham.
> Green fees.
> Green peas.
> Red, yellow, blue, green ...
> Green with envy.
> Little green apples.
> Green light.
> Green beans.
> Green tomatoes
> Green olives

---

[6] The students actually generated many more words than are in the following lists. The student who volunteered to keep a written record got caught up in the excitement.

Like popcorn in a microwave, the students fired off noisily, slowed, then petered out. "Keep translating," I beseeched, "or we *die! How Green Was My Valley!*"

Grass. Green grass.
Green behind the ears.
Greenville, North Carolina.
Bowling Green.
Green Bay Packers
Greenbelt
Greens. Eat your greens.
The Greening of America.
Green cheese.
Greenhorn.
Greenhouse.
Greenland.
Evergreen
Greenup
Greenbacks

Silence. "DON'T STOP NOW!" I implored. "Green, green, green .... Put a spin on the word. Turn it sideways. Put it up against things. Go somewhere with it. Take a language leap!

The green berets
Green Eggs and Ham
Pistachio nuts
Spring
Bananas
Money, Greenbacks
Emerald green
Wood
Army greens
Village greens
Green garden snake
Greenery
Snot
Green frogs
Lollipops
Vomit
Green Grow the Rushes, Ho ...
God Didn't Make Little Green Apples
Greenbriar Resort

When silence eventually prevailed, I grabbed a flag from its holder on the wall, turned it point-end toward the students and shot them dead, rat-a-tat-tat. Now, when I want students to entertain a word's multiple meanings (or hear them groan!), I have only to reach for the flag or better yet, write the word *green* on the board.

Putty This!

To give students a "putty good feel" for word operations, give each a small piece of silly putty and ten minutes of play time. After several moments of stretching, squashing, folding, dividing, flattening, and tearing the putty to pieces, students will extend operations, globbing the putty onto themselves and others, throwing it, and eventually, patching it on to other putties and objects.

When things have gotten "putty much" out of hand, ask students to make a list of putty operations, things putty can *do*. Then write a word, any word, on the board and instruct the students to play with the word as though it were "putty in the hand,"[7] splitting itself, adding itself on to itself, grafting itself onto other words.

Or, give each student a word (a noun) on a 3 x 5 card, divide the students in groups of seven or eight and ask each group to arrange its collective words in a sentence. Students may operate on the words by playing with the words' letters, multiplying, adding or subtracting its "abc's."

To increase language facility and knowledge of word play, assign a project requiring students to put a word of their own choosing through at least ten (the more, the better) linguistic operations. Operating in the grammatological mode, a word can:

Erase or cancel itself
Extend itself
Subtract itself
Repeat or interrupt itself
Show itself literally
Translate differently
Separate at the semes

---

[7] For other ideas, see "Play: From the Pharmakon to the Letter" in *Dissemination*, especially pages 168-171.

Copy, imitate, or parody itself
Allude to itself
Pivot or turn
Show its root metaphor
Graft itself onto another word
Distribute itself as a seed
Move through its various themes
Branch laterally
Represent itself mathematically
Explore its resemblances, valences
Insert itself textually
Re-mark itself
Quote itself

The project which follows, written by a sixteen-year-old female
student and reproduced here in its entirety, makes use of the list to write
the story of "K[NO]W."

K[NO]W

you know who
you know when
with you, of course!

know is a strong word: it breaks down

know> K+ + no(g) + w-
$K = 39.1, N = 14.0, 0 = 16.0, W = 184$
$Know = K + N + 0 + W = 39.1 + 14.0 + 16.0 + 184 = 253.1$

WON= 214, since
KNOW is 253.1,
winning isn't everything

$NO = N + 0 = 14 + 16 = 30$

is know worth more than no? Perhaps
it is more valuable to be able to say

"I know" than it is to say "no"
in complete ignorance.

in the no?
    refusal
know way?
    street inhabited by intellectuals
noledge?
    ledgeless
know excuse?

KNOW KNOWS NO DUE TO ITS INSCRIPTION IN THE
KNOW

Why isn't the reaction affected?

This is simple, clearly an illustration of Le Chatelier's principle as it
applies to inert gases.

WHAT????

If one asks the question, will
this reaction be affected by
the addition of an inert gas,
follow my process. You know it,
don't you?

NO, IT WASN'T MY FAULT.
NO, IT WASN'T MY FAULT.
NO IS ONLY A WORD. A WORD
THAT LOSES ITS POWER AT
THE HANDS OF VIOLENCE.
IT SERVES TO REFUSE INANE
THINGS LIKE "SECONDS" ON
THANKSGIVING, BUT WHEN IT
REALLY COUNTED FOR ME, NO
SERVED TO DO NOTHING. NO,

I AM NOT PROMISCUOUS. NO, I
WASN'T WEARING PROVOCATIVE
CLOTHING. AND NO, I DIDN'T
ASK FOR THIS TO HAPPEN.[8]

It's easy. An inert gas is blah, blah
and blah. Therefore, it hydrajuxtanilopizes
as it is added; do you follow me?

                    NO!

Here, as the reaction occurs, the
pronilitamoliosis takes place simultaneously.
No, you're beginning to see, right?

                    NO!

The pronilitamoliosis cancels out the
belidric effect of the inert gas,
and since green pigs swim in yellow
pools — the answer to the question
I poses would be ...
Do you understand?
                    NO!

Exactly. I knew you would understand
and figure the answer out for yourself.
No, the reaction would not be affected.

knowledge is frightening, but enlightening.
no slams doors SHUT.
know OPENS doors.

---

[8] The exercise was distributed over four standard-size sheets of paper held together by a pink
paper clip. This section, however, was written on a fragment of toilet paper and inserted
between sheets three and four.

The only way I - - - - how to do this is to try. - - - -
advances are made when you work with only what you - - - -.
Although it is difficult, one must explore

new frontiers; - - - - pain, - - - - gain! y'- - - -?

Activities or projects requiring extended word play generate more understanding of language operations than any number of readings in theory. The effect of the exercises is that students experience meaning as a *function* of word play. While playing, students learn how language plays; they learn that words play with words, refer to themselves only as words, contain no reality other than themselves as signs, even if written, like the words of Jesus in some *Bibles*, in red.[9]

Sentence Play

> *The Fish-Footman began by producing from under his arm a great letter, nearly as large as himself, and this he handed over to the other, saying, in a solemn tone, 'For the Duchess. An invitation from the Queen to play croquet.' The Frog-Footman repeated, in the same solemn tone, only changing the order of the words a little, 'From the Queen. An invitation for the Duchess to play croquet.'*

> — Lewis Carroll, *The Annotated Alice...*, 79-80

> *Writing is that **play** by which I turn around as well as I can in a narrow place: ....*

> — Roland Barthes, *Roland Barthes,* 137

"A writer," Barthes writes, "is not someone who expresses his thoughts, his passions, or his imagination in sentences, but *someone who thinks sentences (The Pleasure ...* 50-51).[10] For Barthes, a sentence is not a road taken to arrive somewhere, but a path followed for its "vertical din," the joyous (and enjoyable) interplay of its interstices, the "writerly"

---

[9] Students might regularly "warm up" for class with a five-minute language-operation exercise. In twenty-six class meetings, students could work their way through the alphabet. In the first-class session, they could choose a word beginning with *a* and so forth down the alphabetic line. Or, the teacher could start class by giving students a word (a concept) from a "literary" text to operate on, e.g., the word *green* from *Gatsby*; *sin* from the *Scarlet Letter*; *sublime* from *Frankenstein*; *sprite* from *The Tempest*.

[10] As time and other concerns permit, students might read Barthes' *The Pleasure of the Text* and *Roland Barthes*, works as critical to the understanding of "text" and "textual play" as the Warriners' Grammars are to the understanding of "book" and "closure."

excitement provoked by the play of its parts (*The Pleasure* ... 12). Barthes teaches students to escape the sentence's *sentence* by focusing on its omissions, skips, slides, cuttings, rubbings, collisions, edges, the play of allusions, quotations, all the techniques, in short, language uses to abduct, undermine, and otherwise subvert meaning.

Exercises That Open the Sentence to Play

Exercises like those below help students see the sentence through the eyes of a "Sentence-Thinker," to comprehend it as endlessly configurable as, in Barthes' words, a "*non-sentence*" (*The Pleasure* ... 49). The ideas for these exercises are extrapolated from the texts of Roland Barthes, Gertrude Stein, Julia Kristeva, and Jacques Derrida.

Exercises like those below help students see the sentence through the eyes of a "Sentence-Thinker," to comprehend it as endlessly configurable as, in Barthes' words, a "*non-sentence*" (*The Pleasure* ... 49). The ideas for these exercises are extrapolated from the texts of Roland Barthes, Gertrude Stein, Julia Kristeva, and Jacques Derrida.

Think of the peep holes in protective walls erected around construction sites or "holey levi's." Write a sentence which has no blank spaces but which does have "peep holes." Write a one sentence story about a girl writing a story about a girl writing a story about a fish.

Recall playing a game with friends, a game in which what happens in the play is more memorable than the issue of "who won." Write a sentence in which what happens *in* the sentence is more engaging than its proposition.

Write: I am a fool. Without adding or subtracting a single word or letter, re-write the sentence to cast doubt on the proposition.

Write a one sentence confession of a crime. Without adding or subtracting a word, write the confession again to signify that it was written at the point of a gun.

Write two short sentences. Write a third sentence using the last word of the second sentence to lead into the first

43

word of the first sentence.

Imagine a man or woman wearing a fake pink fur coat, combat boots, large rhinestone earrings, a bishop's miter, war medals, and handcuffs. Write a sentence in which the punctuation, like the accessories, draws attention to itself-as punctuation.

Write a sentence in which the meaning of the word *duck* is indeterminate.

Write a sentence in which the first letter of the first word *kills* the first letter of the next word and in which the first letter of the last word *dies*.

Write a sentence in which ...

Absence figures more importantly than presence
Meaning flickers
Words rain down

Or which ...

Announces a heinous event without naming it
Continually repeats itself, with small differences
Assigns mathematical functions to words
Describes only surfaces, sees only with the camera's eye
Has "an excess of precision, a kind of maniacal exactitude
of language" (Barthes, *The Pleasure* ... 26).
Has blackouts and/or potholes

Students should know that the sentence as a traditional unit of writing is fixed and cannot be commuted, but just as they learn to refinger a musical passage, they can learn, through hands-on practice, to refigure the sentence. As pretexts for these exercises Barthes' own texts are invaluable, but no text can provide the knowledge or insight that comes from practicing or actually "doing" theory.

Experimental Writing[11]: Surfiction

> *Character*: a graphic symbol, hieroglyph, alphabet letter;
> an indelible mark impressed on the soul by the sacraments;
> a set of letters used in writing; the complex of
> accustomed mental and moral characteristics and habitual
> ethical traits marking a person, group, or nation;
> writing, inscription; a piece of printer's type that
> produces a character; position, rank; ...
>
> — Webster's Third International Dictionary

Having "flexed their linguistic muscles," students are primed, eager to write, and in need of suggestions. For ideas linking theory to imaginative practice, experimental texts, if not followed blindly as blueprints or formulas, are rich in possibilities. Ulmer's students, for example, make use of Andre Breton's experimental work on surrealism to produce a fragment of a "false novel." The outcomes of Ulmer's laboratory experiments are not new forms (122) but new insights into the role of the imagination in concept formation (116). Until students realize that the ability to imagine is as "heavily taxed" as the ability to create taxonomies and description, Ulmer argues, we will not be "a truly theoretical discipline" (117).

For stimulating the imagination, Raymond Federman's work on surfiction is also a good resource. In "Surfiction—Four Propositions," Federman theorizes a narrative discourse that invents itself "on the spot":

> ... if the material of fiction is invention (lies,
> simulation, distortions, or illusions), then writing

---

[11] *[Ed.]* The notion of experimental writing has been defined in several different ways in recent years. However, given the emphasis in this chapter on the implications of Derrida's experimental writing for pedagogy, it is useful to note that the term "experimental" is closely related to "inventiveness" for Derrida, as revealed by the following quote in which he writes of the inventiveness of Francis Ponge's little poem *Fable*: "[this writing] is liable to the other, open to the other and worked by it; it is writing working at not letting itself be enclosed or dominated by that economy of the same in its totality, which guarantees both the irrefutable power and the closure of the classical concept of invention. [...] Passing beyond the possible, it is without status, without law, without a horizon of reappropriation, programmation, institutional legitimation; it passes beyond the order of the demand, of the market for art or science; it asks for no patent and will never have one" (Derrida, J. (2007). Psyche: Invention of the Other. In Peggy Kamuf & Elizabeth Rottenberg (Eds.), *Psyche: Inventions of the Other*. Stanford: Stanford UP, p., 46).

> fiction will be a process of inventing, on the spot,
> the material of fiction .... While pretending to be
> telling the story of his life, ... the fiction writer can
> at the same time tell the story of the story he is
> telling ... the story of the methods he is using, the
> story of the pencil or the typewriter he is using to
> write his story .... (12).

For students practiced in alphabetic language operations, Federman's "story of the story" is ideally formulated. It encourages creative (and sustained) use of newly-acquired language skills; it adds additional skills; and it increases the students' understanding of self-reflexivity (the story *as* story, structure *as* structure). Most important, Federman's surfiction models the deconstructionist move: it attacks traditional narrative structure by inhabiting it "in a certain way."[12]

My own students understood Federman's call for a new, self-reflexive fiction, but they had no idea what it might look like. Besides, they complained, they had enough trouble writing with *one* pencil, let alone two, simultaneously.[13] In response to the students' first point, I distributed excerpts from Madeline Gins' postmodern *Word Rain or A Discursive Introduction to The Intimate Philosophical Investigations of G,R,E,T,A, G,A,R,B,0, It Says,* a text written (figuratively) by "two hands."

The narrator of Gins' text provides an example of a character Federman would call a "material of fiction," a "word-being," a "fictitious character committed only to the fiction in which it finds itself, a character which does not simply appear to be what it is, but is what it is, a character as unpredictable as "the discourse that makes" it (12-13). Ginns' *Word Rain* ... is the story, in Charles Caramello's words, of "a woman reading and writing a work-in-progress while being interrupted by a party." True only to her own fiction as a *word*-being, the narrator is both word *rain* and word *reign*. As word *rain* she is weather (warm, misty, capricious, erotic);

---

[12] See Said' s analysis of Derrida's technique of representation in *The World, ...,* pp. 200-203.

[13] To give students the experience of *doing* self-reflexivity, give each student two pencils, one for each hand. Tell them to write the story of a murder with one pencil and the story of the pencil writing the *story* of the murder, with the other.

as word *reign*, she is language (book, custom, fiction). For those unfamiliar with Gins' text, here are several excerpts:[14]

> I appear on a page which would otherwise be blank. I, the mist, the agent, she, appear to swoop you and stratify you, circle you, and synthesize, just as I do now in this short paragraph into which I have fallen ... Notice I am gone.
>
> ....
>
> I give you this book for a present. It comes with a room, light, a country, sky and weather. I will arrange for you to be made aware of these in detail. You may look at everything. You will see only what I see.
>
> ....
>
> In this case a good idea which I have given you is to do the opposite of what I say in spite of yourself: please don't touch the book and no kissing. Think of others before you think of yourself.
>
> ....
>
> Don't read the next paragraph on this page. Forget that you have ever seen this book. Scream for every word you will not see. Perceive nothing. Lose track of me. Kill me. And I hope that I am assured that you will not read between the lines.

Constructing Word-Beings Narrators

The choice of *Word Rain* as a model for Federrnan's surfiction was felicitous. The students fell immediately in love with Gins' playful, textually provocative narrator. "This stuff," they announced, "is cool!" They worked on the narrator's puzzles, followed the labyrinth of her instructions to the letter, laughed aloud at her impertinence. "No matter how many mistakes you make I will hold our breath," Word Rain writes. "I am that which knows what to do." "Anything I tell you, you will listen to," she taunts. "As I speak, so shall you move."[15]

---

[14] The pages in Gin's text are unnumbered. The first quotation appears in Section 4; the second, in Section 1; the third and fourth, in Section 5.

[15] From Section 1.

The narrator's "rain" of words excited the students' textual juices. From Gins, they took the idea of a narrator constructed from the two meanings of a homonym or homophone, a character with a split-text personality.[16] In the two-handed spirit of the project, the students paired off to brainstorm homophones and at the end of the week, presented their word-beings to the class. Not sure of what to expect, I was delighted with the cleverness of the word play, the inventiveness of the "fiction," and the knowledge of language operations.

Several of the texts put materials and objects, as well as words, into play. One story, narrated by the character Cereal/Serial, was inscribed on the backs of cereal boxes flattened and stitched together by yarn (!). The fiction takes place in the morning on the kitchen table. On one level, the plot is the step-by-step (series) working out of a math story problem involving a serial killer; written into the story problem, are mouth-watering advertisements for various cereals (Cheerios, Frosted Mini-Wheats, Rice Krispies); squeals and protests made by the cereals being eaten; the weather forecast from morning television; a "hit list" comprised of names of cereals; a part of a letter refusing, sweetly, a request for a refund on a damaged package of Cheerios. The word-being character in this story is vivacious, funny, and cheeky, in no way similar to the reserved, shy personality projected in the classroom by the girls who wrote it.

Another project took literally Federman's idea of telling the story of the pencil writing the story. The word-being narrator, LEAD/LEAD, is a chewed up, eraserless pencil abandoned on the classroom floor. It is night time and the pencil is writing in the dark on the backs of scrap papers. It is frightened, cold, and lonely, but it has *lead* (graphite) left to give. It understands you deserve more and it has more to offer; it writes you free its headline or *lead* story, an idea for getting rich quick: a self-closing liner for cereal boxes. It has other money-making *leads* to give you; if necessary, it will write all night. The students loved LEAD/LEAD; among other things, it led them to sharing their own ideas for making money. It

---

[16] From cornnents overheard in the brainstorming sessions — "Nah, there's no *play* in that one," and "there's a *lot* you could do with *that* one!" — I judged the students were indeed gaining an understanding of word play.

was a project that in Ulmer's words, tapped the "force" of theory (*Teletheory* 2).[17]

In the same way that Derrida plays with language by moving between parts of speech and miming through "narrative dramatization" (Ulmer, AP 262), students can generate characters for stories about stories by moving through language operations, e.g., lateral associations, skewings, tropic twists, thematic identifications, etymological or analogical relations, anagrams, cross-associations, cross-referencings, or through putting into play, a word with pluri-dimensional meaning, e.g., crossword.[18]

Constructed as an actual crossword puzzle, the character Crossword might be erudite, evasive, tricky, impossible, deliberately indeterminate, obsessed by trivia. Playing on the different forms of the word *cross*, Crossword can show multiple personalities. As an adjective, she might be irritable or petulant, dangerous to cross. As a noun, she might be a crossbreed (language hybrid); a span or ford (transversive or watery); a crucifix (rood, affliction, Little Misfortune). It is of course Derrida's argument that the play of Crossword, the play of *any* word, is inexhaustible, limited only by our own limited understanding of language.[19]

Section 2: Writing Beyond the Alphabet[20]

On prominent display in my classroom is a three-dimensional letter A mounted on a wood platform. The letter's legs are secured to its base by huge nails driven at odd angles into the wood. The *A*'s three cross-pieces, splintery scraps of wood, are lashed with pieces of twine, leather, burlap, and barb wire. The entire project is sprayed fire-engine red. The effect is that of a letter (language) straining against itself, struggling to break form,

---

[17] The project is not to be compared with *Word Rain*, but then Gins does not give you, *free*, her best idea for getting rich quick!

[18] Students would benefit from reading Part I of Derrida's "The Double Session" (*Diss* ... 173-226), a text that contains, in the words of its translator, Barbara Johnson, "a vast panoply of erudition, allusion, and wordplay" (xxvii). Some students may not be able (yet) to "come to grips" with the concepts in "The Double Session," but from Derrida's performance, they will certainly comprehend that words *play*.

[19] In addition to writing surfiction, students might also try writing with split screens (see Derrida's *Tympan*); objective writing (see Robbe-Grillet's *Jalousie*); or framed positionings (see Adrienne Rich's poem, "Frame").

[20] Derrida's idea of non-alphabetic writing, in my understanding, is anything that distributes itself in space, e.g., a series of Papal Bulls, a chain of Pizza Huts, mine veins, varicose veins, funeral processions (274).

but to no avail: The *A* is bound, hammered down, and contained by color, its place in the alphabet secured. The project, an outcome of an assignment to produce a multi-dimensional analysis of a conflict or issue in The *Scarlet Letter*, was widely admired. Students praised its provocative use of materials, its levels of signification, its ability to capture — in one fierce, dramatic gesture — the church fathers' struggle to control the meaning of Hester's sign."[21]

Despite the rigor and challenge of its execution, the project is not the sort of "writing" one would ordinarily expect to find in an English classroom, not even in a classroom committed to the values of postmodern theory. Although Derrida insists that writing exceeds the linear line, that writing, as Spivak explains it, is not writing in the limited sense of a "graphic notation on tangible material" ("Preface" *OG* lxix), the postmodern classroom, like the traditional classroom, continues to privilege alphabetic writing over all other forms."[22]

For reasons that seem patently obvious, the alphabetically inscribed essay will undoubtedly always play a role in the English classroom. If we agree, however, that a teaching practice should practice the theory it teaches, it follows that if the theory teaches that writing exceeds the alphabet, students should write beyond the alphabet. They should have opportunities to inscribe in a "variety of media and styles" (*Teletheory* 5).[23]

Rather than maintain the essay's primacy over all other forms of writing, a postmodern practice will deconstruct the opposition between alphabetic and non-alphabetic writing; it will analyze the implications for

---

[21] The project's meaning, of course, is open to interpretation. Seen through the lens of deconstruction theory, it problematizes the meaning of Hester's action by showing its sign as unstable. A Kristevan lens might focus on the letter's failure to break form as the novel's closure to the play of the semiotic. New historicism might view the struggle to contain the letter (nails, twine, wire) as the attempt of the church fathers to bring sex under the law. "Woman, it is thy badge of shame!" Bellingham tells Hester (hammering, hammering, hammering). "It is because of the stain which that letter indicates, that we would transfer thy child to other hands."

[22] In *Teletheory...* (1989), Ulmer states that discourse analysis research shows "that the privileging of the essay/treatise in school is ideological" (5). Given what we now know about differences in left/right brain activities (some attributable to gender) differences in students' learning styles and methods of cognitive processing, the privileging of the "essay/treatise" over all other forms of inscription is also intellectually outdated.

[23] It is precisely in these investigations of other kinds of writing, Ulmer believes, that the grammatological practice overcomes "the logocentric limitations of discourse" (*AG* 5). In *Applied Grammatology: ...*, Ulmer provides a comprehensive analysis of the implications of Derrida's experimental writing (as opposed to his readings of philosophy) for pedagogy.

a writing understood as "all that gives rise to an inscription in general," including cinematography, choreography, as well as writing that is "pictorial, musical, sculptural" (*OG* 9). As the sculptured *A* suggests, the non-alphabetic project brings a new dimension to the study of theory and, as I hope in this section to show, crosses more boundaries and generates more knowledge than the traditional, alphabetically inscribed essay.

What *Is* Non-Alphabetic Writing?

Having played fast and free with the alphabet, students are primed and willing to write beyond it. First, however, they need to *think* beyond the alphabet, to *comprehend* writing as inscription or "anything distributed in space" (*OG* 9). The concept of non-alphabetic writing is challenging to teach and, as is the case with most postmodern writing, the text of *of Grammatology* does not "teach itself." As an introduction to nonalphabetic writing, I distributed the following assignment:

> Bring to class a writing that is non-alphabetic, one
> constructed by intervals, repetitions, spacing, e.g., land
> inscribed by trees, sand by the edges of waves.

The students stared at the assignment, comprehension not in their eyes. "What is 'non-alphabetic' writing?" they asked. "What are you *talking* about?"

What, indeed? The students were right to inquire. Before distributing the assignment, I should have done what I have been urging other teachers to do: make theory concrete; enact its abstractions; translate its operations into something visible. In other words, show and *then* tell, in that order. It is not difficult, after all, to anticipate the terms and ideas students will need help with; finding the time and energy to present these ideas experientially is, of course, another matter. In response I can say only that like Joyce's ideal reader, the postmodern teacher never sleeps.

When challenged to explain oneself, the best strategy, in my experience, is to seize on something in the classroom domain, an object, device, activity, or scene that embodies the idea. Casting around for an example of non-alphabetic writing, my eyes fell on the classroom windows. Two stories below, I knew, was a playground used in the school's early education program. Aha! I thought. The very *scene* of non-alphabetic writing![24]

"Look down there!" I said, summoning the students to the window and pointing to the playground. "What do you see?

"Nothing."

"Just what you see. A playground."

I grabbed a pencil from a student's hand. "Imagine I am writing on the playground," I said, leaning far out the window, pointing the pencil downward, and making writing motions (loops, crossings, ovals, push and pulls). "What do you see on the playground that corresponds to the movements of my pencil?" "That path!" a student said, indicating the space between the swing and the sliding board. "It's back and forth."

"The see-saw."

"The swing sets."

I turned the pencil on the classroom.

"The chair rows."

"The file cabinet drawers."

"These windows."

At the next class meeting, the students posted on the wall pictures and objects displaying non-alphabetic writing. The pictures included: a tire tread (black-on-white, close-up); five spotted Dalmatians; furrowed farm fields (shot from the air); dancers; a quarter-mile long line of grocery carts, curved in the middle; a cello; a waterfall. Objects included: a dried oak leaf; a pair of madras-print undershorts; a set of fingerprints; a book of matches. From the materials exhibited, I concluded that the students had begun to see beyond the narrow notion of writing as graphic marks distributed on a page to writing as anything distributed in space.[25]

---

[24] Something about the playground's paths and "worn spots" led me to recall Derrida's observation that although Levi-Strauss valued the Nambikwara as "non-writers," the nomad tribe did *in fact* "write," that although the track of the "crude trail" or *picada* they traversed was barely distinguishable, like writing, it *inscribed* itself in the space of "reversibility and of repetition" (*OG* 107).

[25] My own contribution was a typed passage from *Dissemination*, " ... it also inscribes *above and beyond* that movement the very movement and structure of the fan-as-text ... " (251), taped onto a large red fan taped onto a larger-than-life size poster of Madonna posing with

Ideas For Writing Beyond the Alphabet

> *What remains to be developed ... is a genre capable of*
> *sampling at once the archives of the family, the school, and*
> *popular culture. This genre, in other words, is designed to*
> *facilitate the postmodern process of 'crossover', joining*
> *areas of culture that until now have been held apart as if*
> *autonomous.*
>
> — Ulmer, *Teletheory*

From the moment students comprehend writing as anything distributed in space, they see (and report seeing) writing everywhere, e.g., fence posts, six packs, lunch lines, birds in a row.[26] What students need at this point, is a framework for bringing both alphabetic and non-alphabetic writing simultaneously into play, a project that makes use of "everything that gives rise to inscription," or that, in Ulmer's words, samples at once "the archives of the family, the school, and popular culture." In my own classroom, the idea for a "crossover" project such as Ulmer describes came straight from the trash can.

The Senior text

The all-important senior year of high school is constituted by the play of non-literary texts: forms of all sorts, "Graduation Checklists," "Prom Alerts," graduation protocols, P.A. announcements, transcript and ticket requests, measurements, "Senior News briefs," letters of recommendation, and the unending circulation of college-related letters and materials. One spring, rather than ignore these materials (that fall every year from notebooks, pockets, and back packs, overflowing the trash can and littering the floor), I asked the students to collect and weave them into a new writing, called, for want of a better title, "Senior text."

---

her hands spread fan-like on opposite shoulders. Unhappily, the poster was purloined by a Madonna fan (no pun *intended*).

[26] This new grasp of writing as "anything inscribed in space," does not automatically rid students of the conviction that the books read in "English class" are "in a class above" those read at the beach. Although theory has deconstructed the opposition between literary and all other texts, in the classroom, as Zavarzadeh and Morton observe, the literary text continues to receive top billing ("Theory ..." 9). The *idea* of the literary text as discrete and special may no longer control *academe*, but the literary *text* does; its ubiquitous, manifold presence in the classroom still dominates and tyrannizes students.

Emphatically, as I explained in the Senior text description below, I did *not* want the project to turn into a scrapbook:

> A senior text is not a scrapbook. A scrapbook is mindless; it knows only one way to organize itself, chronologically, around certain recurring "time-honored" themes and events. A senior text, on the other hand, has a mind: it *deliberately* misunderstands the "difference" between a an Ivy League application and a prom invitation, a scholarship offer and a putt-putt score. It values equally the thick letter and the thin, the letter of acceptance and the letter left on the street.

The example of the "putt-putt score" was intended figuratively, to emphasize a point. I did not expect to find in the senior texts, scores of *games*. From the example of the "putt putt" score, however, the students took license to include in their projects, texts gathered from all aspects of their senior year experience, non-alphabetic as well as non-literary. In their projects, writing pertaining to graduation and college applications "rubbed edges" with writing having, traditionally, nothing at all to do with the classroom. Below, in alphabetic order, is the "field of texts" one senior class put into play:

absence bulletins	letters
athletic event programs	library notices
autographs	license plate numbers
awards	locker combinations
baggage claim tickets	magazine covers
bank statements	marriage contracts
beer caps	medical prescriptions
bills	medical records
birth certificates	menus
birthday cards	movie ticket stubs
book covers	nail polish colors
bottle caps	newspaper clippings
campaign literature	notebook covers
cap and gown receipts	notes from friends
car repair estimates	parking permits
car repair manuals	parking tickets
cereal boxes	paycheck stubs
certificates	phone bills
church bulletins	poems
class notes	prom programs
college application materials	receipts for disks
compositions	recipes
concert programs	scantrons

condoms
dental appointment reminders
directions to parties
draft registration notices
dried flowers
examination schedules
fabrics from gowns
grades
graduation announcements
gum wrappers
homecoming souvenirs
hunting permits
interim notices

school calendars
school menus
school newspapers
shopping lists
snake skin
song lyrics
spa memberships
speeding tickets
sports numbers
ski-lift tickets
standardized scores
television guides
ties
work permits

The first projects took the shape of oversize books, variously bound and covered. Some covers were quite elegant, utilizing silks and moires embellished with hand-stitched bows, sequins, ruffles, lace. One showcased a portrait of the writer in a wedding gown; the portrait was framed by bits and pieces of the actual gown. Other covers made uses of the United States flag, sports shirts, a Chesapeake Bay Fish House work apron, stuffed animals, tapestries, a pair of jockey shorts, stuffed.[27] Not one project resembled another and not one displayed a "scrapbook" mentality.

Each project wove its own syntax. Some were organized randomly, e.g., drawer or waste can "dumps." Others made use of concealments, juxta positionings, unfoldings, splicings, overlappings, folds, creases, dead ends, stitchings, mirror writing, fragments, white spaces, margins. Some featured popups, cameos, foils, textured fabrics, aromas, decals, stickers, directional signals, superimposed comments, fragments of dialogue, lipstick impressions, P.S.'s, illuminated borders. Several introduced new categories of classification, e.g., ticket collections (speeding, prom, concert, sales); registrations (draft, animal, vote); scores (basketball, songs, SAT scores, first grade report cards).

The so-called literary text, when present, served as a thread in a fabric dependent on other, non-literary, threads for effect (a dependency, of course, the "literary" text would like to conceal). Not Ulmer's ambitious

---

[27] Projects in ensuing years have been less "book bound, 11 due, perhaps, to the purging of the word *scrapbook* from the project description. Now, projects present themselves in forms too various to describe here, e.g., a "text-desk" sculpture, constructed of materials taken from grades K-12; a dance performed under a canopy of texts dangling on strings suspended from the ceiling; a miniature-collection box displaying miniature texts.

"mystery" (*Teletheory* ... 82- 112) nor a Barthesian "circling" (*The Pleasure* ... 34), the project nevertheless did deconstruct the distinction between literal writing and writing that is "alien to the order of the voice" by showing that the distinction, as Spivak writes, is not "rigorous," that one "slips into the other, putting the distinction under erasure" (Spivak, *OG* lxix).[28] Beyond that considerable accomplishment, the projects achieved an excellence, a richness of invention beyond any I have experienced in the classroom.

Activities that deconstruct the literary / non-literary opposition

In the spirit of the senior text project, students might select and share (individually or through a class collage) a significant text from their personal archives, e.g., an excerpt from a letter or diary, a letter of eviction, a letter of recommendation or reprimand. (I would share a copy of my eighth-grade report card on which I received *A* for English, *C* for Behavior, and *D* for penmanship). The project shows the literature classroom as interested in texts of all shapes, colors, and sizes, especially those constituting the students as effects of their own textual histories.

The project might also take the form of a field trip, not like the one taken by the students in the film *Dead Poet Society* to the school courtyard to march to the tune of a "different drummer," but to the campus, to raid trash cans for texts. Divided in teams and wearing simulated EPO I.D. badges, students could make a "paper cut" of the campus, searching in restrooms, building lobbies, empty classrooms, parking lots, library study areas, sidewalks and walkways, cafeteria tables, unlocked cars, and so forth, and giving priority to texts trying hardest to hide themselves, the one that have been folded, ripped, or wadded into balls.

Back in the classroom, students can divide the "trash(ed) texts" and working in groups, analyze the flotsam for its textuality and, from a new historicist perspective, for its cultural content. As a pretext for the foray, students might read one of the many Adrienne Rich poems that take thrown-away texts, undelivered mail, and text-fragments as their subject.

---

[28] The moves among and between different models of writing follow Derrida's own moves from text to object, e.g., the move from Rousseau's texts to the matchbox. In the same way, students can learn to move from one model of writing to another, e.g., from a written interrogation of absence in Morrison's *Beloved* to a choreodrama which takes absence in *Beloved* as its subject.

In "Upper Broadway," for example, the narrator is observed "reaching into wire trash baskets pulling out / what was thrown away and infinitely precious" (In *the Dream of a Common Language* 41). Whatever else the project effects, it will raise the students' textual consciousness to a point of no return.

Inventing Postmodern Objects and Apparatuses

Funky (fun) things

With Ulmer, we would all agree, I think, that "the imagination is an integral part of thinking" ("Textshop," *Reorientations* 117), but only Ulmer, to my knowledge, reports teaching students to use theory to create objects and apparatuses. In the surfiction project described earlier in the chapter, students use the "two faces" of the homonym, e. g., serial/cereal, to create a text narrated by characters with multiple or split personalities. Homophones, puns, and other language plays can also actualize as objects that display two meanings of a word, not as a text character or "word being" but for want of a better term, a *funky(fun)thing*, an object that embodies the word at the root or literal level of meaning.

Most students welcome the all-too-rare opportunity (in an English class) to put words in their place, literally. I will not soon forget the day when, moments before the start of class, a student tore excitedly into my room, brandishing an unrecognizable object. "LOOK AT THIS"! he commanded, shoving the object into my face. "A LIGHTBULB!" Planted in dirt packed firmly into a GE light bulb package was a flowering hyacinth bulb to which the student had attached a short "on-and-off" chain. For a week, the flower flourished on the ledge of my classroom window. When it died, I experienced a sadness only a postmodern teacher could understand.

One homonym, *dyed/died*, embodied itself as a bleeding red tie-dyed T-shirt impaled on a large, crudely-fashioned wooden knife. The funkiest(fun)thing, however, was a *real/reel* apparatus combining both alphabetic and non-alphabetic writing, the brainchild of two male students. To construct the project, the students wrote word-plays on the homonym *real/reel*, cut the text of their script into strips, taped the strips end-to-end to form a fishing line, then wound the line on a *real* fishing *reel*. When unwound, the fishing line reads as follows:

Reel and Real writing joseph goldberg and aaron smith.
Reeling from the blows of reality, reeling in the fish of
hopelessness, quixotic with respect to the reales in her purse,
dancing a Virginia Reel merrily through the reeling twilight,
real to real. Real though it may have seemed, it reeled through
the reels of unreality. A real eel bit Al on the l. REAL DEAL
HEAL MEAL NEAL PEAL SEAL TEAL VEAL WEAL ZEAL The
real deal: a
teal seal named neal ate veal as a meal with weal and zeal at the
healing peal of the bell. As she sat back to watch the fishing
instruction video in her VCR and listened to her 8- track, she was
seized by the need to perform a traditional Irish folk dance.
R=200 E=70 A=l L=30 (these values having been assigned to
their Hebrew equivalents). R+E+A+L= 401=TA (again the values are
derived from the ancient Judaic numerology). R-E-A-L=99=MAIL IS
YOUR MAIL REAL/REEL? Res=thing Realis=of things BUT THINGS
CAN BE UNREAL—CAN 2744 YEARS OF LATIN ETYMOLOGY
BE WRONG?
Hrehulaz=to make a weaving motion Hreol=a spool BUT REELS OF
ALL KINDS ARE USED TODAY MOSTLY FOR THE PURSUIT OF
PLEASURE AS
OPPOSED TO THE HARSH NECESSITY OF SEWING
GARMENTS. REEL EEL
FEEL HEEL KEEL PEEL Peeling the eel she had caught on her reel
from her keel her heel could feel the reel of reality. REAL
ACTUAL FACTUAL SUBLUNARY EXTANT PRESENT
PERCEPTIBLE TRUE GENUINE AUTHENTIC CORRECT EXACT
MATHEMATICAL, while, on a less comic
note, REAL JIG CASSETTE STAGGER HORNPIPE.

Whether seen as language at play or language run amuck, the *real/reel*
project does show an understanding of language far beyond that normally
found in a secondary or undergraduate classroom. The idea for the project
did not pop, like Minerva, full-grown from the students' heads, but from
the classroom *practice* of theory, from exercises and activities that lead
students carefully through increasingly complex levels of play.

Planting a Garden of Postmodern Delights

> *Mistress Mary, quite contrary,*
> *How does your garden grow?*
> *With cockle shells, and silver bells,*
> *And pretty maids all in a row.*

— Mother Goose

As this chapter has repeatedly argued, students in a postmodern classroom should have many opportunities to tinker and play with language, activities and assignments that invite them to paint, nail, sculpt, erect, wire, mold, chisel, or, as in the project below, to *garden*. Impudent, zany, absurd, a postmodern garden is the perfect project for dreary winter days when spirits lag and spring seems far away.

"What this class needs," I announced one February morning, "is a garden, a postmodern garden. Let's cover the board with newsprint and grow flowers!"

The students groaned. "Oh, no. Not more pictures from magazines!"

"Not what I had in mind. Think! What might a 'postmodern' flower look like?"

"A tulip with two lips!" a student exclaimed.

"Smack smack!"

Students never lack for ideas. Using a mix of letters from the alphabet, newsprint, and $15.00 worth of Elmer's glue, they created the terrain from which the garden would grow. They then planted the garden with textual inventions (described below), adding postmodern flourishes and features. As the Catalogue of Contents suggests, no word-processed paper, however wittily argued, has quite / the play power / of a flower.

Mary Alice Delia

A Postmodern Garden: Catalogue of Contents

Flowers: A Tulip: A flower with a two-lips pink blossom and stalky green paper legs covered with pictures of lips cut from magazines. On one of the lips is a picture of the project's creator.

A Buttercup: A butter wrapper planted in a styrofoam cup

A Flour Flower: A paper flower planted in Gold Medal flour

Tissue Flowers: A blossom shaped by tissue wrapping paper imprinted with delicate, colorful, tiny flowers

A Planted Flower: A paper blossom inscribed with pictures of potted plants

A Stalk: A shiny green square stalk, laminated, framing a shiny black blossom, also laminated.

Day Flowers: A bouquet of seven identical red paper flowers, each named for the same day of the week

Birds & Bees

A Bluejay: A set of white paper wings attached to a large feathery J" cut from blue paper

A Bumblebee: A bee with black stripes and wings cut from the text of a New Yorker short story. Each "foot" clutches a tool: pickax, hammer, chisel, the sign of the female, a book titled *Derrida*.

A Bumblebee: A bee whose body is shaped by the letters P L A Y and whose "play" is to throw, with its two front paper feet, a paper ball into a paper basketball hoop

A Robin: A paper robin wearing a black cut out mask and flying with a large rifle between its feet

Absence was in the garden, playfully signified by holes dug into the soil and "alerted" by absence signs. Arrows directed visitors into graffiti-inscribed, dead-end mazes. Words played on themselves, colored themselves, cut *into* themselves, but as the postmodern garden teaches, access to reality is denied at every level. The word *flower* can write itself as *flour* but it cannot, itself, produce a single marigold or zenia.

....

What other postmodern concepts, one wonders, might students give form to? If encouraged to look closely at language, to follow its moves, literally, what other operations might students be challenged to embody or show? Recently, in an article on theory, I came across the words "in the wake of deconstruction."[29] Closing my eyes, I tried to imagine the effect of that ''wake." Would you believe I saw fields littered with letters, *t's* with their tops sliced off, *o's* flattened like Pillsbury Dough Boys?

---

[29] I continue to look for the article in which this expression appears. [*Ed.*] Although this is just a speculation, the author might be referring here to a quote from the book *The Wake of Deconstruction* by Barbara Johnson, published in 1994. In this book, Johnson asks whether deconstruction is dead or alive, and discusses the misinterpretation of the writings of theorists such as Jacques Derrida and Paul de Man.

Mary Alice Delia

CHAPTER THREE
Foucault's Challenge to Pedagogy

One of the most exciting developments in the study of literature has been the rise of new historical analysis. The question remains as to how we will use that analysis to vitalize literary education.

— Brook Thomas, *The Historical Necessity*

At 2:25 p.m. on Thursday, December 23, 1993, I grabbed my coat and my car keys and headed for the parking lot and a two-week winter vacation. On the way out, I circled by the front office for a quick check of the mail room. In each box was a single delivery, a letter printed on light green holiday paper and bearing the salutation, "Dear Colleague." The letter, unsigned, is reproduced below.

Dear Colleague:

Here are a few New Year's Resolutions you may want to think about:

1. I will *not* let students out of my classroom to go to their locker, the bathroom, or the water fountain unless it is an absolute emergency. After all, part of our job is to prepare them for the future and that means teaching them to plan ahead. They have five minutes between classes which should be enough time to take care of most of their needs and allow them to go to class on time with proper planning. Besides, if all of us let just one student out of our classroom at the same time, there would be approximately 60 students out in the halls without supervision. Do I want that? Isn't what's happening in my classroom important enough to keep students in for it?

2. If I do feel it's *necessary* to let a student out of my classroom, I will be sure that student has a pass.

3. I will *not* let tardy students into my first period class, without a note from the Attendance Office, even if they are only a minute or two late. I realize that the only way the school can adequately supervise student tardies to school is to keep a record of them as students sign in. To ignore that is to be irresponsible.

4. I will stand at my classroom doorway between classes, as often as possible, to help monitor student activity in the hallway and to be available should a student or colleague need assistance. Besides, it's kind of fun greeting students as they enter and makes for a more positive atmosphere in the classroom.

5. I will *not* let unexplained student absences pile up in my grade book without following up on them. I understand that I am responsible for students assigned to me during my class periods and it is incumbent upon me to keep good attendance records. Besides I realize that in order to change behaviors, sanctions, both positive and negative, must come swiftly, not at the end of a grading period.

6. I will *not* ignore student tardiness to class. I realize that when students know they don't have to be in class before the bell rings, they won't be in class before the bell rings, and that leads to students feeling the class is not that important. If I act like I don't care about my class, why should the students?

7. I will *not* let students stay to finish a test of mine at the expense of their next class. I realize that to do so is unfair to my colleagues as well as to the students who will miss valuable class time from their following class.

Let's remember that we are all part of a team here. When we work together, everyone benefits.

Have a wonderful holiday and a safe and happy New Year!

Foucault, like Derrida, reads a text like a bloodhound; Foucault, however, does not pursue the same quarry. Derrida reads for the play of signification; Foucault, for evidence of power relations.[1] Rather than deconstruct texts, Foucault uses them, as Dreyfus and Rabinow put it, "as clues to other social practices," both as histories and as *instances* of the discourses which form current power relations (114). For Foucault, the language of the literary text has no intrinsic merit; its value lies in its

---

[1] Threading vs. Mapping: An activity to help students visualize the difference between Derrida's approach to the text and Foucault's. To "materialize" Derrida's concept of the text as a fabric, display an old sheet on the wall and put volunteers to work pulling or "worrying" threads through the sheet's fabric. To show Foucault's view of the text as a location in the history of power and power-relations, display a collage of maps of different time periods and places. Blindfold volunteers, give them magic markers, and ask them to circle locations on the maps. Then ask them to open their eyes and "connect the dots. " Foucault, of course, travels through time and space with his eyes open but the blindfold evokes new historicism's sense of discontinuity, rupture, uncharted pathways, trail-and-error connections. [Props for this activity: sheet, maps, blindfolds, magic markers.]

function as discourse, in its "connectedness" to culture, politics, and the struggle for power. Derrida looks at how language performs as language, as a system of signification. Foucault looks at how language from one field of signification intersects with language from other fields and becomes part of the discourse which Foucault believes constitutes us as human subjects.[2]

Human subjectivity, for Derrida, is a language construct; for Foucault, human subjectivity is a cultural construct, the effect of certain language codes which categorize and classify us according to rules over which we have no individual control. This language is not "objective" or "true" but, like all discourse, is constructed by power relations or more precisely, the use and abuse of power. The link between language and power is not obvious but hidden, and strategies of concealment are the subjects of Foucault's analyses. Foucault's analyses lead to new "grids of intelligibility" or "mappings" and eventually, to the idea that human experience is created and controlled by the language of these "mappings" or what Foucault calls discourse.

As discourse, the literary text both reflects and participates in the language of culture. The literary text not only does not transcend culture; it contributes to the rules or codes which govern cultural practice and which, according to Foucault, constitute us, at any given time, as subjects.[3] Based on this new view of literature as culture-text, literary

---

[2] For a sampling of new historicist concerns and issues, see *The New Historicism*, ed. Veeser. For an overview of new historicist theory, see *A Reader's Guide to Contemporary Theory*, 3rd edition, by Raman Seldon and Peter Widdowson (Lexington: UP of Kentucky, 1993).

[3] Most undergraduates define the word "literature" by offering canonical titles, e.g., *The Odyssey, The Great Gatsby, Grapes of Wrath*. To find out what other assumptions students harbor about "literature," use an "anonymous" checklist like the following:

Directions: Place an A beside statements you agree with and a D beside those you do not. There are no "right or wrong" answers, only individual perspectives and opinions.

1. ___ Some books have more literary merit than other books.
2. ___ A classic is a book that has survived the test of time.
3. ___ Literature reflects society. It does not create society.
4. ___ There is something special about the language of poetry.
5. ___ In this class, students learn how to read and write about literature.
6. ___ A book can use language that is offensive to some people—and still be a great work of art, e. g, Huckleberry Finn.
7. ___ It is possible to be wrong about a book's meaning.
8. ___ A great book contain great truths.
9. ___ Hemingway's anti-semitism has nothing to do with the fact that he is a great writer.
10. ___ Reading is a private, not a social experience.

scholars are now asking new questions. Rather than inquire into what the literary text signifies (as a single, autonomous work of art), critics now want to know what cultural uses are made of it. They want to know how the literary text is promoted, reproduced, circulated; what conflicts or social issues contextualize it, what ideology it supports or represses, what codes it enforces, what material exchanges or links with non-literary texts it tries to hide, what social behaviors it sanctions or punishes. The same questions new historicist critics bring to the literary text, they ask of themselves as readers constructed by culture and historically positioned.

As a philosopher, historian and critic, Foucault has given literary scholars powerful new techniques for reading texts and through the example of his own pedagogy, radically new strategies, methods, and materials for the classroom. One major implication of Foucault's pedagogy for practice is the focus on cultural analysis rather than the literary text *per se*. In the traditional English classroom, work begins with the formalist analysis of an isolated, autonomous book, e.g., *The Scarlet Letter*. In Foucault's pedagogy, the analysis of *The Scarlet Letter* begins with an interrogation into its role in the construction of mid-nineteenth century discourse.

What issues were important in nineteenth century discourse can be seen in the language of nineteenth century institutional discursive practices i.e., in political, medical, legal, religious, educational, architectural, and military documents; in newspapers, recipes, price-lists, ship's logs, title deeds, letter collections, philosophical treatises, manuals, protocols, codes, charts, blueprints, parish registers and in the materials of countless other "signifying" practices. The idea of the literary text as primary-or of the non-literary text as secondary-is the first casualty of a Foucauldian pedagogy.

Beyond the challenge to change the focus of the traditional English classroom, Foucault's pedagogy entails new methods of presenting concepts and materials. Most writers on Foucault, for example, concede the stunning effects of his scenes; they are histories, Hacking states, that "stick in the mind" (30). Whereas Derrida's classroom opens slowly, with questions about syntax, margin, translation, and the practice of what

---

Record the number of A's and D's for each statement. To open discussion, focus on statements with which most students agree.

Said calls the "technique of trouble," Foucault's classroom opens abruptly, without pretext or preamble, onto scenes marked by the graphic depiction of torture, death, and dismemberment.

To see Foucault's visual method in action, we need only turn to the opening of *Discipline and Punish*, where the *scene* of power is powerfully *seen* as power over the body, power to mutilate the body, to hack it down, draw and quarter it, tear it limb from limb:

> On 2 March 1757 Damiens the regicide was condemned 'to make the *amende honorable* before the main door of the Church of Paris', where he was to be 'taken and conveyed in a cart, wearing nothing but a shirt, holding a torch of burning wax weighing two pounds'; then, 'in the said cart, to the Place de Breve, where, on a scaffold that will be erected there, the flesh will be torn from his breasts, arms, thighs and calves with red-hot pincers .... (3)

No one who reads this passage will think the texts of Michel Foucault, however variously understood, should be taught dully or in ways that circumvent their power to disturb. Foucault's visually provocative description of Damiens' torture is instructive not only of his thesis but also of methods of teaching that thesis. One lesson the scene offers is that a Foucaldian pedagogy makes compelling use of, and new interpretive demands on, the eye. The scene of Damien's torture and death, for example, is the scene of power powerfully *shown* as the power to punish. Although Foucault's relation to the visual is complex, there is no doubt that "visual astonishment" is one effect of reading Foucault's texts (Martin Jay, "In the Empire of the Gaze" *NH* 178). Many of Foucault's ideas, in fact, uniquely *depend* on striking images ·or what Hacking calls "brilliant before-and-after snapshots" for their effects (29).

The scene "has always haunted Foucault," Deleuze observes (*Foucault* 80), and without doubt, Foucault would be among the first to agree. "Spatial obsessions," Foucault writes, "have indeed been obsessions for me." "But," Foucault continues, "I think through them I did come to what I had basically been looking for: the relations that are possible between power and knowledge" ("Questions ..." 69). In addition, then, to a new focus on the relation of literature to culture, a Foucauldian pedagogy will appeal directly to the eye. Foucault's scenes are intended as texts; they are not meant to "illustrate" or "clarify" or "enrich" cultural analysis but to show power at the moment of use (or abuse), to show power as the power to discipline, as power over the body. To the degree that Foucault's scenes disturb and assault the senses, they are concerned to *show* power-in-action; like the pictures on posters in post offices, Foucault's scenes fight against power's abuses by showing its face.

Other than the appeal to the eye, Foucault's scene is silent. Instructively, Foucault does not interpret the material he shows us but simply presents it, letting it enact its own historical voice. Although brilliantly lit, his scenes contain no subtitles or footnotes, no faces or "authors" we recognize. As readers, we naturally look for meaning in the scenes, but it is Foucault's strategy to thwart that desire and let the histories perform their own dramas. The payoff is that we *see* things a "deep meaning" theory would conceal or shape differently. In the details of Damiens' execution, we *see* power exercised openly as power over the body. In the details of Foucault's description of an early seventeenth military institution, we see power exercised as surveillance: "'A company street is fifty-one feet wide ... All tents are two feet from one another. The tents of the subalterns are opposite the alleys of their companies'" (*Discipline* 171).

Analysis is not absent from Foucault's work, but in a Foucauldian classroom, the eye is primary. It is not the case, as Deleuze writes, that in Foucault "analysis and illustration go hand in hand" (*Foucault* 24). The visual in Foucault is not intended to "aid" or "illustrate" (in the sense of clarifying or enriching), but to provide a point of departure, an opening, if you will, for the show of discourse.[4]

In addition to its "show first, tell later" methodology, Foucault's pedagogy models new time / space mappings and juxtapositionings. As his readers well know, Foucault's texts are characterized by rapid reorderings of materials, sudden shifts in perspective, chronological jumps, detours, stepbacks, zoom-ins, and other non-traditional reading maneuvers. With the skill of a high wire artist, Foucault leaps from one grid of intelligibility to another, from the concrete to the abstract, from the past to the present, from a single event to a set of institutional procedures,

---

[4] [*Ed.*] Contemporary scholars have analyzed the relationship between *sayability* and *visibility* in Foucault in terms of a "visual discourse analysis." Traue et al. (2018) explain this notion referring to "visual agency", "With Foucault, we understand visibility to be a material condition that is not outside society (representation) and not inside the subject (competence, habitus), but which exerts its agency through working itself deeply into the fabric of social action.)" (Traue, B., Blanc, M., & Cambre, C. (2018). Visibilities and Visual Discourses: Rethinking the Social With the Image. *Qualitative Inquiry*. https://doi.org/10.1177/1077800418792946).

from the 1857 execution of Damiens, for example, to a set of rules drawn up in Paris, 1837, for the governing of young prisoners (*D&P* 6). Derrida "moves us into the text," Said writes, but Foucault moves us "*in* and *out*" (183). Foucault's sweeping trajectories take away the breath but open the eye to what otherwise would remain invisible. In its preoccupation with cultural analysis and archival materials, its willingness to cross discourse boundaries, its use of the visual, Foucault's pedagogy marks a new way of "doing business" in the English classroom.

This chapter argues that although we cannot, obviously, teach every lesson in the manner of Foucault, we can learn from Foucault to do more than we *are* doing to communicate the excitement of his project. The first section contains activities for introducing cultural analysis and for raising students' awareness of its power to shape human experience. The second section presents a rationale for selecting the school institution as a first object of study. The next section explores the use of visibility and examination as institutional disciplinary mechanisms. The fourth (and longest) section shows how school documents can function in the classroom as texts for discourse analysis. The fifth section contains ideas for moving discourse analysis from the classroom to culture-at-large.

Like the last chapter, this one is not a closely knit set of procedures but a mix of school discursive practices (including student-generated materials), critiques of traditional classroom procedures, institutional forms, narrations of class sessions, newspaper clippings, ideas for presenting ideas, and ideas for activities and projects yet to be undertaken. Because the materials are familiar to high school students and undergraduates, they provide a convenient starting point for discussion.

Section 1: Introducing Culture Analysis

> *In this case, student experience has to be first*
> *understood and recognized as the accumulation of*
> *collective memories and stories that provide students*
> *with a sense of familiarity, identity, and practical*
> *knowledge. Such experience has to be both affirmed and*
> *interrogated.*

> — Henry A. Giroux, *Liberal Arts Education...*

As defined by Websters, culture is the set of "concepts, habits, skills, art, instruments, institutions, etc. of a given people in a given period." For Stephen Greenblatt, new historicism's preeminent professor, culture is politics, a "poetics" of practices and assumptions that "functions as a pervasive technology of control, a set of limits within which social behavior must be contained, a repertoire of models to which individuals must conform" ("Culture" 225). For the new historicist classroom, culture, cultural analysis, and cultural understanding are the new objects of study. If literature, as Greenblatt writes, is now "the servant of cultural understanding" (227), the new pedagogical goal is "to establish links between the text and values, institutions and practices elsewhere in the culture" (226).

Certainly, the introduction to a theory as culturally focused as new historicism should generate an interest in culture, provide opportunities for class culture exchanges, prepare students to read the literary text as a cultural document, and show students how culture constructs them as individuals. Following Giroux's imperative to begin where students *are*, I ask students to make a list of television shows, toys, games, cartoons and candy that figured importantly to them as children but that have now disappeared. Here are the lists generated by one class of seventeen-year-olds in the spring of 1993:

Cartoons	*Toys*	*Games*	*Candy*
G.I. Joe	Big Jims	Atari	Tutti-frutti
He-man	Bionic Woman	BMX	
Popeye	G.I. Joe (old)	Chutes & Ladders	
Robo Tech	Gobats	Twister	
Silver Hawks	Garbage Pail Kids		
Spiderman	He-man		
Superfriends	Match Box		
The Littles	Pound Puppies		
Thundercats	Rainbow Brite		
Transformers	Sit/Spin		
Voltron	Voltron		

Television shows

A-Team	Facts of Life	Love Boat
Air Wolf	Fat Albert	Mork & Mindy
Alice	Gidgette	My Martian
Benson	Good Times	One Day at a Time
Brady Bunch	Great Space Coaster	Too Close for Comfort
Different Strokes	Happy Days	What's Happening

Students love the journey into their own cultural history. It licenses sentiments otherwise held in check (especially by males), affirms experiences school typically exclude, and provides opportunities for students to bond. In remembrance of things past, students reach (not so far, for them) into closets, shelves, drawers, all the while remembering, forgetting, sharing, questioning. ("Oh, oh, oh, what was the name of…?" "Uh uh uh … *you* know, the one that...") Memories are jogged, laughed at, confessed. ("I used to..."). Information is exchanged ("I wasn't allowed to..."). Questions of interest to theory are posed ("What happened to...?" "Why did they change...?").

The activity also encourages students to think critically about the ways in which their own social/cultural expectations have been shaped by the media, especially (for this group) television shows like "The Brady Bunch" and "Fantasy Island." ("I thought families were *supposed* to be like 'The Brady Bunch' and I never wanted to invite anyone over." "I thought there really *was* a "Fantasy Island.") Because the discussion is intense, students remember and allude to it throughout the course. Activities that are memorable give students a grammar or "short-hand" for the quick dispatch of ideas.

71

Mary Alice Delia

Cultural Analysis of a "School" Text: The Prose Anthology

> *Course readings certified by inclusion in the confines of*
> *an anthology seem available to exegesis or admiration but*
> *not to manipulation or critique; the teacher as the*
> *authority stands with the anthology, certifying it as a*
> *repository of meaning; the student reader/writer,*
> *without a hope of ever being anthologized, can only*
> *retreat into the powerlessness of trying to say the right*
> *thing, thereby pleasing the teacher and honoring the*
> *anthology's contents.*

— M. H. Dunlop, *Practicing Textual Theory*, 252

While the fiction anthology has become a site of cultural contestation, the prose anthology, even less open to women and minorities, draws less critical fire. One reason may be that the prose anthology uses a multiplicity of screens and juxtapositionings to conceal its racial and gender bias, e.g., interspersing short, "representative" passages by women writers in sections devoted primarily to longer selections from "important" white male writers; "padding" the numbers of women and minority writers represented by an indexing system which "counts some writers twice."[5] Students can do a "quick cultural check" on the anthology, however, by identifying cultural issues it excludes. Before opening the anthology, ask students to generate a list of topics important to them personally but absent from the anthology's Index. According to a class of high school seniors (1994), the following topics (arranged in order of listing) are inadequately represented in the 1992 *Norton Reader*, an anthology used in both secondary and undergraduate classrooms.

> abortion, homosexuality, murder in the urban streets, stress, rebellion,
> criticism of American government, drugs, abuse, hemp legalization,
> rape, hitchhiking, unemployment, racism (violator's point of view),
> eating disorders, gambling, cheating, science fiction, assisted suicide,

---

[5] *The Norton Reader* (Eighth Edition, 1992), uses multiple indexes to cross-reference and reposition titles and writers ("Contents" and "Index of Rhetorical Modes and Strategies"); interpolates mini-collections with major sub-divisions and uses vague, meaningless titles ("History," "People, Places"); and draws fire from male-dominated sections by assigning them "less major" headings. "An Album of Styles's" sixteen entries, for example, includes only one woman writer, Virginia Woolf. All "heavy mental" sections are dominated by male writers: "Ethics's" sixteen essays include only two by women; "Science's" eleven, only one; "Philosophy and Religion's" thirteen, only two.

gossip, prejudice against Latinos, virginity, HIV, clothing styles, mental and physical handicaps, military violence, masturbation, condom distribution in schools, abstinence, making money, life after death, teenage sex, gun control, affirmative action, animal husbandry, crime committed in other countries by Americans.

Finally, nothing in the *Norton Reader* touched on the question: "If you like to eat ice, are you sexually frustrated?"

Culture and Bloomingdale's: The Bridal Register

JENNIFER AND DAVID HAVE CHOSEN THE LAURA ASHLEY STYLE (ENGLISH OR FRENCH COUNTRY) FOR THEIR DECOR.

THEIR TOWELS ARE CANNON ROYAL TOUCH IN WHITE OR CAPTAIN'S BLUE/SLATE; ALSO, CENTENNIAL TOWELS IN TEA/ROSE ENGLISH ROSE.

JENNIFER'S OVERALL COLORS THROUGHOUT THEIR HOME ARE
VARYING SHADES OF BLUE (FROM NAVY TO DUSTY BLUE) AND TEA ROSE (ENGLISH ROSE).

THEY ARE REGISTERED AT HECHTS, WOODIES, BLOOMINGDALE'S AND MACY'S.

— From a Shower Invitation, 1991

Of all the documents students examined in a course focused on cultural analysis, the bridal register yields the greatest number of insights and elicits the most interest. A goldmine of cultural goods, materials, and practices, the register shows "culture in action" in all areas of human economy. Copies of bridal registers are easily obtained from major department stores and can be xeroxed for use as a class text. Before reading the registers however, students should generate their own. In the act of actually constructing a register, they *register* culture's role in shaping their expectations.

I divide my own class in "engagement pairs" consisting, where possible, of one male and one female.[6] To tap the "cultural unconscious,"

---

[6] Crackerjack, dimestore, or student-made wedding rings add a special dimension to this activity.

I allot each pair *no more than* five minutes to complete a list of goods and services they consider indispensable to a marriage. The list below (reproduced as submitted), although not a traditionally formatted register, shows a cultural "bottom line" for two eighteen-year-olds contemplating marriage in a certain location in America in 1994.

> waffle iron, vacuum cleaner, refrigerator with ice-water dispenser, capuccino machine, china (white), tablecloth (white), stereo, VCR-VHS, cable subscription, projection screen TV, dishwasher, washer-dryer, pool cleaner for pool, curtains, leather couch, lazy boy chair, craftmatic II adjustable bed, beachhouse in Hawaii, tupperware, kitchen pots & pans with teflon, microwave, two cars (Lambourghini, Ford), ceiling fan, salad shaker, piano, plants, *Rolling Stone*, *Time*, *Newsweek*, seeds and other garden stuff, video camera.

An item-by-item interrogation of "Bridal Register" lists helps students understand what cultural analysis is about and shows them culture's role in constituting a certain "lifestyle" or way of living.[7] To give students the opportunity to express their own views of the role of culture in shaping human experience, I ask them to respond (agree or disagree) in writing to the "Letter to the Editor" below (or one like it).

> The Vice President is correct that the Murphy Brown character is an example of certain values in today's society (at least the white, professional upper middle-class society). But he is wrong if he thinks Murphy Brown is influencing the values of American society. Murphy Brown may in some ways be a role model, but it is only because she already was a role model before she was ever created. Murphy Brown is a *product* of a value system, not a creating force. Successful television shows (and movies) reflect values and value systems; they do not create them. Television shows that do not reflect the ever-changing but oh-so-constant values in American society are unsuccessful. Television is the way it is because people are the way they are, not the other way around. You can't blame the mirror for the problems of the reflection.
> Martin Pippins, *Washington Post*, May 30, 1992: A19.

---

[7] Another suggestion is to ask the same pair of students to write a marriage contract. To show students their own cultural assumptions about gender, switch to a divorce scenario. Who gets what? Why?

Section 2: The School as First Object of Study

Asked in a 1976 interview about his silence on the subject of geography, Foucault replied: "One can perfectly well not talk about something because one doesn't know about it." In the same interview (see excerpt below), Foucault emphasizes the role of practical, real-life experience in his own historical work. He began with a genealogy of psychiatry, he explains, because he had personal knowledge of the psychiatric hospital and was involved with its "combats" and "tensions." Later in the interview, Foucault observes: "If I do the analyses I do, it's not because of some polemic I want to arbitrate, but because I have been involved in certain conflicts ... "(65). Although Foucault's stated objective is "to create a history of the different modes by which, in our culture, human beings are made subject," his choice of topics reflects interests that are current and personal (Foucault, *Afterword* ... 208). Foucault seldom counsels; for that reason, I quote at length his comments on the subject of where to begin historical work:

> To me it doesn't seem a good method to take a particular science to work on just because it's interesting or important or because its history might appear to have some exemplary value. If one wanted to do a correct, clean, conceptually aseptic kind of history, then that would be a good method. But if one is interested in doing historical work that has political meaning, utility and effectiveness, then this is possible only if one has some kind of involvement with the struggles taking place in the area of question. I tried first to do a genealogy of psychiatry because I had a certain amount of practical experience in psychiatric hospitals and was aware of the combats, the lines of force, tensions and points of collision which existed there. My historical work was undertaken only as a function of those conflicts.
> ("Questions ... "74")[8]

For the same reasons Foucault began his study of the human sciences with a genealogy of psychiatry, teachers and students, I believe, should begin with the school, where they have practical knowledge of the power relations which constitute their everyday reality, access to discourse documents, and where they have an immediate "stake" in the matter. Foucault's own interest in the school as an object of discourse analysis and reform is well documented. Although he never wrote a full-scale

---

[8] From an interview with the editors of *Herodote*, a French radical geographists' journal.

history of the genealogy of education, the school is never absent from his analyses and in May, 1968, Foucault himself undertook "revolutionary action" against it.[9]

Foucault was a practical philosopher. He understood very well that although all institutions are subject to critique, not all are equally open to intervention. In a 1971 discussion sponsored by *Actuel*, Foucault was asked if he intended to intervene in the asylum. "That is a task for psychiatrists," Foucault responded, "since entry into an asylum is restricted" (*Revolutionary Action ...* 228-229). The attack on psychiatry, Foucault suggests, could better be carried out in areas and activities increasingly influenced by psychiatry, e.g., "social workers, professional guidance counsellors, school psychologists." Asked where he planned to act, Foucault replied:

> We would like to work with students in the lycee, those whose education has been supervised, anyone who has been subjected to psychological or psychiatric repression in their choice of studies, in their relations to their family, in their response to sexuality or drugs. We wish to know how they were divided, distributed, selected, and excluded in the name of psychiatry and of the normal individual, that is, in the name of humanism. (*Revolutionary Action ...* 229).

Foucault's response provides a compelling argument for beginning historical work in the school and especially, the *high school* where, as Foucault observes, repression mechanisms operate openly as normalizing procedures. Although repression exists at all levels of education institutions, it is most visible in the high school where the violence of its effects, as Foucault's interviewer reports, is experienced in "the most immediate way" (218). In a public-school institution, as in a hospital, military camp, or prison, students are subjected to constant surveillance, scrutiny and discipline. From the moment they enter the school building until they depart its grounds, they are tracked, scanned, examined, tested, evaluated, grouped, isolated, experimented upon, detained, and subjected to search, punishment, and a host of micro-penalties and fines. In the same way that Foucault's analysis of the prison makes visible strategies of containment at all levels of the justice system, an analysis of disciplinary power exercised openly in the high school reveals how discipline works at all levels of education. Because the high school "even more than the

---

[9] Foucault demonstrated on behalf of the students in the May, 1968 rebellion and was arrested by the Paris police.

university" has a "full range" of power mechanisms, an analysis of its discourse yields a more comprehensive understanding of the link between power and knowledge (225).

Section: 3. In the Eye of the School: Visibility and Examination

> *Take for example an educational institution: the disposal of its space, the meticulous regulations which govern its internal life, the different activities which are organized there, the diverse persons who live there or meet one another, each with his own function, his well-defined character—all these things constitute a block of capacity-communication-power.*

— Foucault, *Afterward: The Subject and the Power*, 218-219

In "The means of correct training" (*Discipline and Punish* 170-194), Foucault looks at the school as the site of a power that depends on the techniques of visibility and examination for control. Because students recognize the practices Foucault writes about, as the account below shows, they are quick to understand the relevance of his critique.[10]

"This school *is* built like a prison! Listen: '... the rooms were distributed along a corridor like a series of small cells.' That's what our classrooms are, cells! And the cafeteria—it's sunk down so the teachers can look down on us at lunch." "Get this! A 'perfect eye' (173).[11] That's what Ms.___ has. I swear, she sees through walls."

"Look at this! 'Latenesses', 'absences', 'inattention', 'disobedience', 'incorrect attitudes.' Hey, I've had detentions for every one of those!" (178).

"What does 'compulsory objectification' (189) mean?" a student asked (189).

"Foucault believes that knowledge produced by the 'human sciences' is not 'scientific' or objective. If knowledge were objective, prison guards, teachers, social workers, counselors would eventually be out of a job. To perpetuate themselves, the great institutions of research and study

---

[10] Selections included pp. 172-174, 177-178, and 187-189.
[11] Page numbers are to *Discipline & Punish* (See Works Cited).

must constantly construct knowledge, psychiatry must construct new mental illnesses, educationalist must construct learning disorders."

"How do they do that?"

"Through a process of objectifying human behavior; by observing human behavior, quantifying it to produce norms, and then identifying individuals who are 'deviant' or operating 'below norm.' Since the norms are perceived as 'objective', the institution can use them to examine and prescribe treatment for individuals. If 98% of all people get up on the right side of the bed in the morning, for example, then the 2% who get up on the left side, obviously, get up on the *wrong* side. These wrongsided individuals are identified, examined, counseled, and forced to undergo therapy or treatment.[12]

"Oh God."

"Wowwww."

"Geez."

Following up on Foucault's analysis of the school's use of visibility as a disciplinary mechanism, the students toured the school. As they walked, they noted the placement and distribution of passageways, restrooms, classrooms, doors, teacher and student desks, windows and intercom systems, partitionings, security guard locations, communication control devices, and other architectural and positioning strategies schools use to control students by rendering them visible.

Following the tour, the students drew diagrams showing the exact location and reach of the surveillance techniques which, taken together, comprise the school "Eye."

---

[12] To dramatize how education "scientists" collect the information they need to construct new knowledge, show scientists in the act of "suctioning." Use a syringe type cake-decorating tube to "draw" information from the head of a student volunteer.

Section 4: Reading School Discourse

State and Local Attendance Policies

I will be present in school every school day. I will not be absent for any reason including illness. If I do not feel well, I will report to school. Ms._____ will determine my status.

— From an Individual Student Contract, dictated by the school's principal, effective April 5, 1990

Because state attendance policies affect students directly, we began our analysis of school discourse by reading the 1988-89 Maryland State School Attendance Policy.

> According to state regulations, absences from school for the following reasons are lawful and shall be excused: Death in the immediate family; certified illness of the student; court summons; work or activity accepted by school authorities; observance of religious holiday; quarantine; physical and mental incapacity; violent storms; state emergency.

Radicalized by their reading of Foucault, the students tore into the text: "Who decides all this stuff, anyway?"

"What gives the state the right to decide what's lawful and what's not?"

"Does this mean if I cut class I'm a criminal? I could go to JAIL?"

"What if you don't *have* an immediate family?

"I worship the sun. Does this mean I can go to Ocean City any time I want and have it excused?"

:)

Next, we looked at the local school student handbook. In addition to republishing state attendance regulations and policies, the handbook contains language requiring students to maintain a full schedule of classes:

A student must have a class, study hall, or aide assignment for every period of the day unless an alternative program or reduced schedule has been approved. No student may have a 'free period.'

To show the school's obsession with attendance, I shared with the students a memorandum directed to faculty requiring students to remain in their seats, bell-to-bell.

At the end of the year, it is vital to stand tough on your attendance policies. Don't release students from class.
Don't let them quit and stand by the door at the end of class.
— From Instructional Council Meeting notes, April 27, 1989.

"What is everyone so afraid of?" a student asked. "They treat us like children. What do they think we're going to *do*?"

"This place is a PENITENTIARY!"

"Worse." I said. "A penitentiary sees everything; the high school can't, so it lies awake at night in a cold sweat, worrying about the blind spots. In the morning, it writes more memorandums."

Finally, we looked in the student handbook at micro-penalties attached to attendance:

Students enrolled in a school-approved work program may not work any day they do not attend school.

Students who are absent from school may not attend any school activities (e.g., play, basketball game) on the day they are absent without prior administrative approval.

"This is ridiculous!" the students protested angrily.

"What if I'm sick in the morning but feel better in the afternoon? Why can't I go to work?"

"It doesn't make sense. It's like your mom saying if you don't pick up your room, you can't use the car."

"School doesn't make sense, man. They have all these little-bitty ways of controlling you. I can't wait to get out of here!"[13]

---

[13] :)

School Observation & Report Forms

Not only are prisoners treated like children, but children are treated like prisoners. Children are submitted to an infantilization which is alien to them. On this basis, it is undeniable that schools resemble prisons ...

— Gilles Deleuze, *Intellectuals and Power*, 210

Historically, in the high school as in other institutions, power is exercised as power over the body. In my own school days, students who misbehaved were hauled into the principal's office and paddled with the "board of education." At that time corporal punishment was just beginning what Foucault describes as its long journey underground: before removing the paddle from its hook, the principal lowered the green shade over his office door.

Today, the "board of education" has been displaced by an educational board, a network of quasi-medical practices in which discipline operates openly as reform or treatment (*D&P* 104-131). In my own school system, so-called "problem" students are the province of an Educational Management Team (EMT), a committee comprised of an administrator, a counselor, and the school nurse. Although infinitely more subtle than the principal's paddle, EMT operations are no less effective as a disciplinary apparatus. Few students know of its existence and fewer still know the role classroom teachers are compelled to play in its "processing" of students. As the form below shows, the EMT's power lies in its ability to construct students as objects of its own quasi-medical discourse.

SECONDARY TEACHER REFERRAL/REPORT[14]

Student's Name _____ I.D. No._____

School _____

| Section I | Complete A or B only |

A. EMT Referral
Form Completed by:

_____

Report discussed with parent?
___Yes ___No
Date Discussed: ___
(Attach parent conference notes related
to reasons for referral)

B. Purpose of Report (Check one)
__ ARD Screening
__Annual Review
Progress Update

Form Completed by:

_____
Name   Date

Section II

Reason for Referral/ Report, including summary of student's strengths and weaknesses. Attach pertinent work samples:

Check any interventions you have used:

___ Student Conference
___ Adjusted workload
___ Counselor involvement
___ Behavior management
___ Note/ Call to parents
___ Parent conference
___ Disciplinary reports
___ Tutoring (peer, volunteer)
___ Modifying methods, materials, and presentation
___ Change of text/materials
___ Change in schedule
___ Consultation with specialists
___ Consultation with colleagues
___ None

Explain which interventions were most effective:

Other Comments:

---

[14] Documents pertaining to students "officially" diagnosed as "learning disabled" are perhaps more yielding of power/knowledge relations, but for students new to new historicist theory, the behaviors described in the "Referral Report" are instructive.

BASED ON YOUR OBSERVATIONS, PLEASE EVALUATE THE STUDENT IN COMPARISON TO OTHER CLASSMATES BY CHECKING PROBLEMS FREQUENTLY OBSERVED.

ATTENTION/ORGANIZATION ACTIVITY LEVEL

___ Difficulty maintaining attention
___ Easily distracted
___ Loses or forgets work and/or materials
___ Late for class
___ Underactive
___ Overactive
___ Difficulty with organization

DAILY WORK

___ Difficulty taking notes
___ Does not attend class regularly
___ Incomplete homework assignments
___ Poor test grades
___ Does not complete in-class assignments
___ Does not participate in class

SOCIAL/EMOTIONAL

___ Interrupts and distracts class
___ Lacks motivation
___ Sudden changes in mood throughout the day
___ Lacks self-control
___ Inconsistency in performance
___ Needs constant approval
___ Unusually aggressive towards others
___ Unusually shy or withdrawn
___ Difficulty interpreting social cues
___ Does not accept responsibility for own behavior
___ Easily influenced by others
___ Easily frustrated
___ Does not get along with adults

Although not credentialed to treat or manage "deviancy," teachers *are* authorized to identify students who, in the teacher's judgment, exhibit deviant behaviors. To the degree students depart from classroom norms (which, according to Bourdieu's analysis in *Distinction*..., merely reproduce the values of middle-class culture), they are subject to treatment and remediation. An analysis of the form's language shows the influence of psychiatric discourse on school discourse and the school's use of "psychiatric knowledge" to "manage" the student body. That the

Educational Management Team's intent is to diagnose and treat students for something in excess of the "Three R's," is shown in the fact that more than half the form's categories deal with social and emotional behaviors, areas that traditionally speaking, have nothing to do with academics.[15]

Another school normalizing disciplinary apparatus is the "Interim Report to Parents" (reproduced below), a form mailed mid-marking period to parents of secondary students in danger of failing. Lacking a theoretical basis for challenging the "Interim Report's" language, students find its discourse difficult to penetrate. As a new historicist point of departure, I ask them to identify the items *most* and *least* related to academic performance. Then, to show the report as a report on the *family*, I ask the students to identify words and phrases implicating parents as well as students.

INTERIM REPORT TO PARENTS

___ Make up tests

___ Make up quizzes

___ Make up homework

___ Arrange for help on, or further explanations of assignments & objectives

___ Participate more in class activities

___ Spend more time on the work

___ Keep records or notes

___ Improve study skills or work habit

___ Pay close attention in class

___ Socialize less in class

___ Come to class with necessary materials

___ Complete work on time

___ Get to class on time

___ Attend class regularly;

___ Class absences this report period

___ Other _____

_____

_____

Signature,
Teacher

---

[15] One of the EMT's disciplinary mechanisms is the "Daily Progress Report," a form which designated students must carry *on the body* and petition each of their teachers, each day, to complete and sign.

___A conference is desirable. Please contact the school to arrange this with me and/or a counselor.

___If this box is checked, please sign and return.

I have reviewed the Interim Report with my child.

_____
Signature, Parent

The items students find most related to academic performance are make ups, tests, quizzes, and homework. The items they find least related are those pertaining to classroom behaviors, e.g., socializing, participating, paying "closer attention" and so forth. The item students feel most implicates parents is the attendance report. In bringing attendance to the parents' attention, the form implies that parents have failed adequately to supervise it, that parents, too, are delinquent. The school's surveillance in attendance areas constitutes what Foucault would call one of the "lateral controls" by which schools discipline and control parents as well as train "docile children." "The bad behavior of the child, or his absence," Foucault writes, "is a legitimate pretext" for the school to infiltrate and supervise the home (*D&P* 211).

Yet another form used by schools to discipline students is the "Appeal for Restoration of Credit." Students in most school systems are permitted a specified number of unexcused absences per semester course; when the number is exceeded, students lose course credit. Credit lost in this manner can be restored only if the student appeals in writing to the teacher and only if the teacher accepts the appeal. Unsigned, the letter of appeal provides an excellent text for the analysis of school discourse; those reproduced below are typical in that they offer an explanation for the absences and a promise to "improve" class attendance.

THE APPEAL FOR RESTORATION OF CREDIT

Dear_____:

This essay has been written to appeal my loss of credit in your class. After reading this essay, I hope you will understand why I lost credit and hopefully restore credit.

The reason I lost credit in your class is due to the fact that I have had too many unexcused tardies in your class. I'll admit I do have a problem getting to school on time. Normally my mom drives me to school, but before she can do that, she has to drop off my little sister at the bus stop. My little sister, _____ goes to school in_____, and her bus stop is not even within walking distance. Some of my unexcused tardies however are due to my problem with getting up early enough to catch the school bus.

In the past I've also been very negligent about this. I never really thought about what the consequences would be if I lost credit.

If my credit is granted, I promise that I will try my hardest to get to school on time. I'll also do my best to improve my grade in your class.

In the future I will try to improve my habits. I'll try to get up earlier to catch the school bus, participate more, and pay more attention in class.

Hopefully after reading this essay, you can give serious thought as to whether you will restore credit or not. Hopefully you will decide to restore credit.

_____

Dear_____:

There is one reason and one reason only for which I have lost credit; that is due to five unexcused absences.

I deeply regret losing credit and I am very remorseful. I realize that I was irresponsible and made unwise decisions.

Yet, I would greatly appreciate it if my credit were to be restored for reasons due to my high academic performance in Narrative Drama I.

I was off to a bad start at the beginning of the second
semester. At interim time I was failing Narrative Drama I. By
the end of the marking period, I had managed to pull my grade up
to a "C. " The following marking period I was determined to do
well. From then on, my grade stayed a stable "C." Many times, I
was the only student to do my homework in my class.

It is late in the school year and too late for me to be on a
contract. But if there are any special conditions or
requirements, I am willing to follow them.

Please consider restoring my credit. Thank you for your time and
patience.

Sincerely,

_____

Although the letter can be used in class in a variety of ways, I usually
ask students to identify words or phrases that refer to areas other than
academic performance, e.g., "unexcused tardies," "negligent," "pay
attention," "if credit is granted," "remorseful," and "irresponsible." The
letter can also be used as a basis for an improvisation in which students
role-play as teachers and student petitioners. In one version, the teacher
summons the student petitioner to his/her office for a conference; in
another, the teacher solicits advice from colleagues or, in a more formal
context, participates in one of several panels of teachers convened to pass
judgment on requests for restoration of credit.

Discourse varies according to the school's type, level, and location,
but all institutions of learning, kindergarten through the university, govern
through statements permitting them to affix micro-penalties. Although
less concerned to "track and treat" than the high school, colleges publish
rules, procedures and penalties pertaining to tuition payments, entrance
requirements, dormitories and residences, class attendance, general
deportment, departmental and graduation requirements, political
correctness, in addition to procedures for obtaining parking permits,
maintaining athletic eligibility, dropping and adding courses, requests for
graduation materials, transcripts, letters of recommendation, and so on.
Where possible, the texts of these institutional forms should be distributed
in the classroom and read along with *Discipline and Punish* and the so-
called "literary text," e. g., *The Scarlet Letter*.

Section 5: Reading Beyond School Discourse

Eventually, students reach beyond school discourse to read discourse in the culture at large, cook books, for example, church bulletins, advertising, government publications, and especially, first, second, and third class mail.[16] One piece of mail that outraged a class of graduating seniors was a twenty-four page booklet titled "Play It Safe in Ocean City" published by a coalition of national, state, and local drug and alcohol prevention groups, and, beginning in the spring of 1993, distributed annually, via the school, to seniors throughout the state of Maryland. While most of the booklet is devoted to emergency telephone numbers, discount coupons, and advertisements for hotels, restaurants, and places of entertainment, the booklet opens with the following letter of "welcome."

```
TOWN OF OCEAN CITY
Mayor & City Council
P.O. Box 158
Ocean City, Maryland 21842

REPLY TO:

Office of the Mayor
P.O. Box 158

Dear Graduates:


We are very pleased to welcome you to Ocean City this summer.
You will find everything here to entertain you ... sun, sand,
sea and plenty of fun. We know that you will take advantage of
all that Ocean City has to offer.

You do need to be aware of your actions and those of your
friends. Like your hometown, Ocean City has rather strict rules
and ordinances which govern conduct. Most of these—like noise,
public drinking, trespassing and destruction of public property—
```

---

[16] [*Ed.*] This notion of "reading beyond" clearly appeals to the pragmatic dimension of discourse, which cannot be fully captured through a linguistic analysis and involves, instead, the broader cultural framework. This broader dimension is merged with human tendency to interpret reality in the form of discourses, even when the starting material is non-linguistic at all (e.g., we hear a car engine starting sound in the night and interpret it as "Paul got into a fight with his wife"). A few words are sufficient for humans to build a story, as shown by the famous six-word story attributed to Ernest Hemingway, "For sale: baby shoes, never worn."

have their origins in the 'golden rule' and can be followed by
applying good common sense to your actions.

It is important for you to know, however, that the City will not
tolerate destruction of public or private property, public
drunkenness nor displays of hostility toward public institutions
or officials. Our police officers will enforce the law.

Again, we are delighted to have you as our guest. Please treat
others as you would like to be treated and we know you will have
a great time.

Sincerely,

_____

Mayor

Chairman, Ocean City Drug and
Alcohol Abuse Prevention Committee

Following the letter is a "wages of sin" list of consequences or "things
that can happen" to students who fail to observe the rules:

Date Rape
Chemical Dependency, Alcoholism
Pregnancy
Sexually Transmitted Diseases
AIDS
Legal Problems
Jail
Injuries
Death

Among other things, the "Dear Graduate" letter provides a clear
picture of how discourse in one jurisdiction makes calculating use of
discourse in other jurisdictions to increase the base of its power.[17] As
implied by the letter's language, the rule governing conduct in Ocean City
is no different from, is *the same as*, the rule governing conduct in the
students' "home" (family) and in the students' home "town" or political

---

[17] To help students understand the concept of multiple discourses, show them a newspaper
article or report in which the word *criminal* (or *crime*) is linked with the word *confess*.
Then, draw on the board the outlines of two buildings: a courthouse (American flag) and a
church (steeple). Ask: "To which of the two buildings should a 'confessed criminal' be
remanded--the courthouse or the church?" Students themselves can look for other
examples of multiple discourses.

jurisdiction. Since rules governing conduct have common origins in the "golden rule" of the church (the admonition to "do unto others as you would have done unto you"), a "graduate" who drinks beer publicly in Ocean City, Maryland, is guilty not only of a breaking an Ocean City ordinance, but also of behaving as a wicked, inconsiderate, and ungrateful child.

To help students see the multiplicity of discursive practices at play in the letter's discourse, ask them to identify the institutional voices that appear in the letter's text. Then, ask the students to draft, for an administrator's signature, a letter addressed to their own upcoming graduates. Congratulatory in tone, the letter's real purpose is to ensure a trouble-free graduation ceremony.[18]

In addition to providing a model for writing discourse, the "Dear Graduate" letter can also serve as a basis for:[19]

A Foucauldian Scene. Ask students to read aloud, without comment, the two scenes which open *Discipline and Punish*: a description of a 1757 public execution and an 1837 time-table.Then challenge them to present the "Dear Graduates" letter in the same Foucauldian manner, as a document or event in the history of penal reform: e.g., a surgically detailed account of an individual's arrest, in 1993, Ocean City, Maryland, for drinking a Miller's Light in public.

An Improvisation. Use the letter's facts as a basis for an improvisation (voiced or unvoiced), with students role-playing the following stereotypes: a bar-keeper, a recent graduate, a police officer, a bystander, a passer-by. Video-tape the improvisation and show it "without footnotes" to the class.

---

[18] To give students more practice in writing discourse, ask them to write a set of rules and regulations governing the practice of jogging. Divide students in groups and assign each group one of the following tasks: (1) Create regulations pertaining to jogging; include rules governing location, time of day, equipment and dress. (2) Determine jogging norms for children, adolescents, adults, the elderly. (3) List conceivable deviations or abnormal jogging behaviors. (4) Design educational programs and precise medical (including psychiatric) treatments for deviant or delinquent joggers. (5) Create posters for campaigns/meetings that depict deviant joggers as anti-social, cultural anathemas, and so forth.

[19] Foucault teaches that power should be studied "from the ground up, at the level of tiny local events where battles are unwittingly enacted by players who don't know what they are doing" (*The Archaeology* 28). "Foucault's genius," Hacking writes, "is to go down to the little dramas, dress them in facts hardly anyone else had noticed, and turn these stage settings into clues to a hitherto unthought series of confrontations ..." (*The Archaeology* 28)

A Mock Trial. On trial: The Graduate. The charge: drinking in public. The penalty: a $3,000 fine and/or three months in jail. Characters, role-played by students, include the Graduate, the Mayor, the Substance Abuse Prevention Committee Chairman, witnesses, a police officer, and whatever other characters students think the scene warrants.

Texts lending themselves to cultural analysis are not hard to come by, especially when students take responsibility for gathering and sharing discourse materials with the class. As students develop in their ability to identify and analyze discourse, they bring materials to class that most teaching practices would deem unrelated to the study of "literature," e.g., calendars, junk-mail circulars, seasonal catalogs, paper place mats, death notices, church fans, car repair manuals, materials found in "non-literary" places, e.g., truck stops, waiting rooms, motel and post-office lobbies, under windshield wipers, funeral parlors, beauty shops, car-repair shop lounges, public trashcans, alley ways, back floors of automobiles, and most recently, pre-formatted computer databases and menus. Nola's *Personal Record Keeper* (Berkeley, California), for example, offers the following 27 categories (and over 200 subcategories) pertaining to family records and files:

1. Emergency Information	15. Credit Cards
2. Available Money	16. What You Owe
3. Sources of Current Income	17. What's Owed You
4. Persons/Retirement Accounts	18. Burglar Alarms
5. Securities	19. Locked Places/Keys
6. Real Estate	20. Hiding Places
7. Business Interests	21. Medical Information
8. Copyrights, Patents, Inc.	22. Memorabilia/Things
9. Vehicles/Boats/Planes	23. Personal Documents
10. Home Inventory/Valuables	24. Personal Information
11. Insurance	25. Your Family
12. Advisors Money/Tax/Legal	26. Death Plans
13. People/Services/Contracts	27. Estate Matters/Will
14. Tax Records	

What students see at first glance in Nolo's *Record Keeper*, is that almost all categories pertain to (or have subcategories pertaining to) material assets. Only one category (Memorabilia/Things) is reserved for items of non-monetary, strictly personal value, e.g., family photos, letters, and mementos. The main menu categories furnish "ready-made" subjects for extended new historicist investigation, e.g., the function of finance advisors in contemporary culture, or issues relating to credit, contracts, copyrights. Space precludes listing the contents of Nolo's 200 subcategories, but one, "Home Inventory/Valuables," contains topics of special interest.

Antiques	Floor Coverings	Photographic Equipment
Appliances	Furs	Precious Metal
Art	Furniture	Rec/Camping Equipment
Bedding	Garden/Yard Items	Religious Items
Books	Gems	Silver
China/Pottery	Guns	Sports Equipment
Clothing	Holiday Items	Stamps
Coins	Jewerly	Tapes/CDs/Records
Collectibles	Live Things/Plants	Tools/Work Equipment
Computers	Musical Instruments	Window Coverings
Crystal/Glassware	Office Equipment	Wine/Liquor
Electronic Equipment	Pets	Other Items, Misc.

Viewing the above list through the "wrong" or distancing end of a telescope, students see a certain strangeness in pairings, e.g., computers/crystal, gems/guns and in the distinctions, e.g., antiques and collectibles. Beyond these pairings, however, are questions about databases as techniques for collecting what Foucault might call the "already-said." The purpose of the categories and subcategories, after all, is not (as advertised) to reveal or show what is hidden in family accounts, but to "reassemble" that which *can* be known or read, and that toward the goal of self-management, or in Foucault's words, of "nothing less than the constitution of oneself" (*On the Genealogy of Ethics* 247).

To sum up, this chapter has explored the implications of Foucault's writing for the classroom and has argued for a practice that centers on culture, uses cultural documents as objects of study, makes new demands on the eye, explains less, reaches further, and, through the use of stagings, demonstrations, improvisations, role-play, and props, *shows* Foucault an renders his ideas visible. The next chapter probes the implications of Foucault's texts for teaching the literary text, for introducing the research project, and for carrying out other classroom discursive practices.

CHAPTER FOUR
Foucault's Challenge to Pedagogy (Continued)

I would like to write the history of this prison... Why? Simply because I am
interested in the past? No, if one means by that writing a history of the past in
terms of the present. Yes, if one means writing the history of the present.

— Foucault, *DP*, 31-32

Using Foucault's teaching methods as a model and drawing on ideas
elaborated earlier, this chapter argues for a new historicist practice that
begins in the analysis of current power relations; reads the literary text as
a history of the present; frames the traditional research project as an
investigative report; explores the use of new formats and presentations;
displaces the journal with the letter; and in a section linking Foucault and
Derrida, interrogates the letter both as discourse and text. Like the last
chapter, this one is imbued with the spirit of play. As Foucault himself
counsels: "Do not think that one has to be sad in order to be militant"
(Hand xlii).

Section 1: The Analysis of Power Relations

In Foucault's "history of the present," Dreyfus and Rabinow observe,
"there is an unequivocal unabashed contemporary orientation" (*Michel
Foucault*: … 119). Although *Discipline and Punish* opens on the scene of
punishment in the past, its story begins in Foucault's analysis of bio-
power relations in prison revolts occurring in his own time. "That
punishment in general and the prison in particular belong to a political
technology of the body," Foucault writes, "is a lesson that I have learnt
not so much from history as from the present" (*DP* 30).[1]

---

[1] Power over the body or "Bio-power," as defined by Dreyfus and Rabinow, "is the
increasing ordering in all realms under the guise of improving the welfare of the individual
and the population" (xxvi). [*Ed.*] The notion of bio-power in Foucault is sometimes
intended more broadly as "power over life," which includes "power over the body." As
specified by Arnason (2012), "Michel Foucault (1926–84) coined the term 'biopouvoir'
('biopower') to describe power as it concerns human life, in particular with regard to the
human body on one hand and human populations on the other. Historically, biopower
emerged with the transformation of power formations in Western societies starting in the

Although Foucault's work begins in the present, with knowledge derived from the analysis of current power relations, in many new historicist practices, there is scarcely a word about the institutions that "discipline and punish" people in real life situations ("Taking Aim... " 10).[2] Students get their first knowledge of power relations from anthologies, from essays that describe power exercised in the past, not first hand, from their own analyses of power relations in the present.[3] Pedagogically (and according to Foucault), that is the wrong way to go. A new historicist inquiry moves from the present to the past, not the other way around. It is the knowledge of power relationships in the present, after all, that arouses interest in or motivates the study of power relations in the past. If the new historicist goal is to read the literary text as the "past" of the present, then students should identify, in present institutional practices, a component, technique, procedure used routinely to gain or exercise power, e.g., drug testing, fingerprinting, community service assignments.[4]

Despite the (seeming) ease with which Foucault isolates power components, most students will find the assignment hard going. The identification of power routines is not, after all, a routine classroom procedure. In my own practice, I use the following activities in combination: the analysis of current power issues as represented by the

---

seventeenth century. Foucault claimed that biopower evolved in two forms, which he called anatomo-politics of the human body, or discipline, and biopolitics of the population. The former is concerned with making the human body useful and docile, the latter with managing human populations. [...] They were distinct in the eighteenth century, but were eventually linked together through a multitude of relations and merged into a coherent, new technology of power in the nineteenth century. [...] The concept of biopower is relevant today for various topics in applied ethics, most obviously for topics related to the cases studied by Foucault: punishment and sexuality. The concept is also highly relevant for a great variety of other topics, for example reproduction, transformation of the body (from genetic and pharmacological enhancement to body-building, cosmetic surgery, and body art), public health, medical practice, biomedical sciences, race, and disability, to name just a few" (Arnason, G. (2012). Biopower (Foucault). In *Encyclopedia of Applied Ethics, Second Edition* (pp. 295-299)).

[2] In "The Confession of the Flesh," a conversation between Foucault and other intellectuals, Foucault defines *institution* as follows: "The term 'institution' is generally applied to every kind of more-or-less constrained, learned behavior" (197).

[3] I am thinking of publications such as the MLA *New Approaches to Teaching...* anthologies; Cambridge University Press' s *New Essays on ...*; and collections such as *The New Historicism*, ed. Veeser, and *Foucault: A Critical Reader*, ed. Hoy.

[4] One of the most provocative questions I have ever been asked in the classroom came from a student who wanted to know why "men seem to go for girls with blonde hair." Questions like these motivate students to undertake the research necessary to "write the history" of the Clairol bottle.

media; the investigation of power relations in real-life situations; and the construction, for classroom display, of discourse collages.

The Analysis of Power Relations as Represented by the Media

One sign of a practice focused on current power relations is a trash can overflowing with newspaper clippings. The five excerpts provided in Appendix A and described below, are but a sampling of the many submitted during recent controversies over college curriculums, art exhibitions, the Anita Hill affair, gay-rights, surrogate motherhood, censorship, smoking prohibitions, abortion, and other controversial issues.

The first excerpt, from "The Dead Sea Scroll Monopoly," speaks to Foucault's argument in "The Discourse on Language" (and elsewhere) that certain rules of constraint control discourse (224), in this case, access to the Dead Sea Scrolls. The second excerpt, "Monday Night at the Temple of Health," and the third, "Hospital is Object of Rights Inquiry," pertain to Foucault's interrogations of the politics and regime of health, especially in essays such as "Body/Power" and "The Politics of Health in the Eighteenth Century." The fourth excerpt," Suspended Students Not Always Sent Home," relates to Foucault's analysis in "The carceral" (in *DP* and elsewhere) of disciplinary exchanges between schools and prisons. The fifth excerpt, "Mom and Dad's Choice," applies to Foucault's analysis of the "medicalisation of the family" in "The Politics of Health in the Eighteenth Century" (172-175).

Because the issues are still current, the excerpts provide convenient window on power and power relations in present cultural conflicts. Periodically, I clip five or six short articles or letters from the daily paper and send them, along with the questions below, to student-technicians in "Foucault's Laboratory" for interrogation. The questions are referenced to Dreyfus and Rabinow's analysis, in *Michel Foucault: ...,* of the following areas of focus in Foucault's work: the "emphasis on discursive formations" (including non-discursive issues); the focus on "rituals of power" (rituals combining knowledge and power); and the "isolation of bio-power," a concept which links "technologies of the body" and "the discourses of the human sciences" (184).

Mary Alice Delia

Foucault's Laboratory

Directions: Identify and label all texts that evidence the following characteristics or behaviors.

__ appear to be open to interpretation (Dreyfus & Rabinow 108)

__ appeal to cultural/societal norms (108)

__ show the body as the place where "local social practices" link with "large scale" organizations of power" (111)

__ reveal the use of knowledge to gain power (120)

__ are governed by fixed but unstated underlying assumptions

__ link disciplinary techniques with the "norms" of a social science (143)

__ show discipline as technique (153)

__ suggest a cultural trend (203)

__ take advantage of differences in economic status, "know-how," traditions, cultural practices (223)

__ show power as the effect of surveillance or physical threat (223)

__ show power as organized (224)

Students need not be actively involved in a specific cultural conflict in order to take it seriously. If, as Foucault believes, culture shapes our identity, then no issue in the culture-at-large is outside, or unimportant to, the new historicist sphere of inquiry.

Investigating Power Relations in Other Institutional Settings

Newspaper and other media can show power's effects but they cannot put students themselves "in the picture" or give them first-hand knowledge of power's components. As a philosopher, Foucault was uncommonly street-smart; his understanding of power came from his struggles against existing forms of power in realworld events, not from the "literature" classroom.[5] In the same way, students should be encouraged to *experience*

---

[5] In "Revolutionary Action ...," for example, Foucault makes reference to his involvement with groups "working in the struggle against repression, in the penal system, in psychiatric hospitals, and in the police or judicial systems" (223)

power's operations, to learn, from any of power's "countless, tiny sources," the specifics of its techniques ("Intellectuals ... " 214).[6] To learn about power students must engage power, if not in the street, then elsewhere, through operations that yield specific knowledge of power's apparatuses, the procedures and techniques it routinely employs to assure survival.

One strategy for investigating current power relations is to ask students to provide detailed accounts, in class, of persistent attempts to obtain, by telephone, letter, or in person, on behalf of themselves or others, information about or entry into, items or areas listed below. The accounts may be narrated (as investigative reports, letters) or re-enacted (role-played) and should, where possible, include transcriptions of verbal exchanges. One effect of the assignment is to show students that "not all areas of discourse are equally open and penetrable; some are forbidden territory ..." (Foucault, "The Discourse..." 224).

Credit rating
Medical file
Personnel file
Psychological test data
Copy of a teacher recommendation
Class rank or academic standing of a doctor, minister, rabbi,
    priest, teacher
Membership in a private club, e.g., golf or country club
Laboratory blood test results (from the laboratory)
Police record of a public-school student
Hospital survival statistics for specified operations
Salary of a department store cosmetic salesperson
Record of complaints filed against medical personnel,
    lawyers, teachers and school administrators, section
    bosses, clergy
Listings of church holdings, properties, investments
Records of bonuses awarded to employees by local retail
    stores, manufacturers, corporations
Permission to attend a meeting of a medical review board
Permission to distribute free paperbacks to patients in
    psychiatric facilities

Confronting power is one thing; analyzing power relations, another. In response to his own question, "How is one to analyze the power

---

[6] Foucault's examples include "a small-time boss, the manager of 'H.L.M.' (modern rental housing), a prison warden, a judge, a union representative, the editor-in-chief of a newspaper" (214).

relationship" ("Afterword ..." 222), Foucault provides both a *caveat* and a concrete approach. First, the caveat. Power relations analyzed from the point of the institution, Foucault points out, privilege the institution and lead to a situation in which power explains power to itself in the same way, for example, as a leopard might "explain" its spots. Because power relations operate both within and without the institution, the institution must be analyzed from the viewpoint of power relations and not, as Foucault writes, the other way around (222).

On the question of how to analyze power relations, Foucault is explicit. He looks at five factors which "*permit one to act upon the actions of others*" (Emphasis mine); these factors, Foucault translates as "points to be established" (223). If possible, students should read Foucault's own discussion, in "The Subject and Power," of the factors involved in the analysis of power relations; if Foucault's text is not available, students might use the questions below (a mix of paraphrase and Foucault's own wording) to analyze their real-life power investigations."[7]

Questions for the Analysis of Power Relations

1. System of differentiations

Are any of the following differentiations in operation?
__ differences sanctioned by law, traditions, status
__ differences based on privilege, know-how, competence
__ differences in linguistics or culture

2. Types of objectives

Are any of the following objectives obvious?
__ the maintenance of privileges
__ the accumulation of profits
__ the exercise of authority, function, or trade?

3. The means of bringing power relations into being

Are any of the following "shows of power" evident?
__ threat of arms
__ effects of words
__ use of economic differences
__ surveillance systems

---

[7] Foucault's scheme for analyzing power relations can be found in "Afterword: The Subject and the Power," pp. 223-224.

__ rules (explicit or not)

4. Forms of institutionalization

Are any of the following institutional mechanisms ev ident?
__ mixings of law, custom, culture
__ authority of closed systems e.g., scholastic, military
institutions
__ use of government (local, state, federal) disciplinary apparatuses

5. The degrees of rationalization

Are any of the following reasons offered as "justification" for uses of power?
__ cost effectiveness
__ certainty of results (end justifying the means)
__ necessity (due to resistance met)

The Display of Discourse

If you allow your dog to defecate in a park, you must pick up the waste and remove it. Pet waste may not be placed in trash cans, whether in a park or at your home. It is recommended that you remove your dog's waste from a park in a plastic bag and flush the waste (NOT the bag!) in the toilet after you return home.

— Fallsmead Forum. April, 1995[8]

The walls of my classroom are papered, literally, with discourse. The story of the decor begins in an antique shop, a site I visit frequently in search of props.[9] On this occasion, I was looking for an inexpensive stereoptican and, as luck had it, I found one and immediately cast about for a stereo-view card with which to test it. To my annoyance, there was not, in the entire shop, a single stereo-view card and I left the shop empty-handed.

Several days later, "casting about" in the classroom for an example of discourse, I came up, again, empty-handed. Frustrated, I determined, like the speaker in Frost's "Provide, provide," to supply myself with samples of discourse to refer to. That night I cut swatches of discourse (samples of discursive practices) from every newspaper, journal, and magazine I could find, accounts of arrests, trials, controversial proposals, awards, insurance and real estate advertisements, job-related announcements and so forth.

---

[8] A monthly publication distributed to selected homeowners, Rockville, Maryland.
[9] The background in this section is intended to provide an explicit account of how, in a new historicist classroom, one idea seems to lead to another.

Next morning, I dragged the gallows from the corner to the center of the classroom, thumbtacked my clippings on its center post, and circled headlines and key phrases with a red highlighter. Drawn to the power of the "apparatus," students read the clippings with interest.

That night, and the next, I cut again. When the gallows' post was covered, I posted on the crossarm, all the way to the noose. To read these clippings, students had to step up on the gallows' base (a step they were loathe to take, considering the gallows' easy-to-operate built in body-drop). As the gap between the clippings and the noose narrowed, student interest in the clippings increased, as did the pressure on *me*, to produce them. What had seemed like a great idea turned into a nightmare of late night rummagings, constant hand-washings, burning eyes, and growing stacks of unevaluated student papers.

In an interview with geographers, Foucault talks about the methodological problem of "material constraint," of the impossibility of one person "covering the whole" of the "spatiotemporal field" (67). Realistically, the mapping of spaces "in question," Foucault says, "would have to be a collective undertaking" (68). With Foucault's words in mind, I enlisted the students' support. In the next several weeks, while I slept, the students papered the room (walls, blackboards, windows, door, ceiling) with pictures and accounts illustrative of Foucault's ideas, especially the concept of bio-power. The cumulative effect was awesome. In the silence that at the end of the day falls over a classroom, I could see and feel, literally, Foucault's description, at the end of *The Order of Things*, of the erasure of man, "like a face drawn in sand at the edge of the sea" (387).

The point here is not the discourse *per se*, but the gathering of discourse for display, the eyeball encounter with words and pictures describing or depicting power and power relations,[10] e.g, "Mercy Killing Not Allowed," "Military Gay Ban," "Officers' Use of Force," "Stiffer Civic Fines," "A Family Bill for the GOP," "The Breast Ban," "Witch Hunt in the Senate." In retrospect, the project might take the form of a new historicist anthology, a collection of disciplinary practices gathered from the students' own culture as well as from culture-at-large, "video-

---

[10] [*Ed.*] Displaying discourse through "papered walls" is a visually effective representation of how human environment is essentially constituted by words (or letters intended as discourses, as discussed below). Please check note 28 for a related discussion.

view" cards for Foucault's stereoptican.[11] Examples of "culture in action" are everywhere and, given the short list of (over-lapping) suggestions below as a jumper-cable and a pair, each, of blunt, child-sized scissors, students should have no difficulty finding and cutting.[12]

> Newspapers, journals, city and county weeklies, including advertisements, especially the "personals."
>
> Signs posted inside and outside of public transportation vehicles, transportation terminals, factories, stores of all kinds, churches, hospitals, prisons, clinics.
>
> Local, state, and federal laws, rules, and regulations, especially those related to exclusions, trespassing, licensing, funding, accountability procedures, penalties.
>
> Institutional publications (schools, churches, hospitals, prisons, corporations, government offices and agencies).
>
> Publications of special interest groups, e.g., American Kennel Club, truckers, retired persons, scouts, fan clubs, sports, computers, and ad infinitum (see Internet's RN).
>
> Photographs of institutionally sponsored degrees, internships, licenses, credentialings, certifications.
>
> Publications of Homeowners' Associations (regulations governing architecture, dues, public areas, pets, etc.)

If the present is, as Foucault believes, the story of power relations, and if power relations are embedded in every societal, cultural, and institutional practice, then there is, in the present, no end to analysis and no shortage, ever of discourse to look at.

---

[11] To raise money for certain reforms, the book might be sold in the local university bookstore to teachers and students in all areas of the human sciences.

[12] To show the pedagogical violence of the assignment, distribute, along with the scissors, the following passage from Adrienne Rich's "On Edges": .... I'd rather/ taste blood, yours or mine, flowing/ from a sudden slash, than cut all day/ with blunt scissors on dotted lines/ like the teacher told" (Leaflets 45) .

Section 2: Reading *One Flew Over the Cuckoo's Nest* as the History of Current Institutional Bio-Power Practices[13]

> *...you boys be good boys*
> *and cooperate with the staff*
> *policy which is engineered for*
> *your **cure**, or you'll end up*
> *over on **that** side.*

— Ken Kesey, *One Flew Over...*, 21

> *Look at the entrance to a*
> *Renault plant, or anywhere*
> *else for that matter; three*
> *tickets to get into the*
> *washroom during the day.*

— Gilles Deleuze, *Intellectuals...*, 210

Most new historicist classrooms read the literary text not, as Foucault, to write the history of power relations in the present, but to map power relations in the past. The new focus on cultural context may challenge the idea of the book as a transcendent, autonomous work of art, but it does not show the connection between New York City's current use of "dog waste patrols" for example, and the mirror wielded in 1955 by Kesey's Big Nurse to check under the rim of the asylum's latrines. Despite Foucault's insistence on the importance of moving *outside* the text, few teachers of new historicism venture the crossing.

To transgress the book's boundaries, one must get past the blurbs on its cover, the first line of post structural scrimmage. Although printed (deceptively) on the outside of the book, they lead (like traditional pedagogies) to the inside, from the cover to the covered: "You've never met anyone like RANDLE PATRICK MCMURPHY," the blurb on the

---

[13] Kesey's novel plays a role in Greenblatt's account of transfers and exchanges among Gary Gilmore and Jack H. Abbott (convicts); Mailer, author of *The Executioner's Song*; and would-be writer, Richard Adan, Abbot's victim. According to Greenblatt, Gilmore, a death-row convict, was "explicitly and powerfully moved by the film version of *One Flew Over the Cuckoo's Nest*" ("A Poetics of Culture" 10-11).

back cover of Kesey's novel promises.[14] McMurphy is depicted as a "lusty, profane, life-loving fighter" who enters into battle with Big Nurse armed only with "his own indomitable will." The focus on McMurphy's "heroism" invites the sort of question Foucault advises us to suspend: What can we learn from McMurphy about how to bring meaning into a meaningless world? ("What is an Author?" 137). What McMurphy knows or does not know is of no interest to Foucault. To Foucault, McMurphy is a "stick figure," a player in a scene that neither he, Big Nurse, or any other of the novel's characters, completely understands. Rather than read Kesey's novel as the story of a free-wheeling agent who "swaggers into the ward of a mental hospital and takes over," Foucault would ask: what can we learn from Kesey's description of a mid-twentieth century psychiatric facility that will help us write the history of bio-power practices in the here and now?

For Foucault, the value of Kesey's novel lies in its graphically detailed depiction of power as bio-power, a power which relies for its survival on technologies of the body. Since the mid-fifties and the publication of Kesey's novel, bio-power technologies and techniques have become so sophisticated, so adept at presenting themselves as the "cultural norm," that diagnosing their operations and/or elements has become increasingly difficult. For Foucault, Kesey's novel provides a "step back" to a time when power operated openly as power-over-the-body and to a place or location for observing bio-power techniques, procedures, and day-to-day operations.

In the activities that follow, students move "back and forth" in time, "in and out" of the text, in the manner of Foucault's trajectories. The interrogation of bio-power opens with activities designed to draw attention to its current "classroom components," the strategies and techniques employed in school institution settings to discipline and control the student "body."

---

[14] New York, Signet: 1962. (The Signet paperback edition was published in the same year as the Viking hardback edition.)

Identifying Classroom Bio-Power Techniques

I will not chew gum in class.
I will not chew gum in class.
I will not choo gum in class.
I will chew gum in class (that's 4)
I will...

"The spider's genius," Adrienne Rich writes, is "to spin and weave in the same action" ("Integrity," *A Wild Patience* 9). Like the spider, the self-reflexive new historicist teacher performs (or attempts to perform) two operations simultaneously: in the moment of interrogating disciplinary techniques in *One Flew Over the Cuckoo's Nest*, she shows herself in the act of disciplining her own class. In the manner of Foucault, she moves "in and out" of the text, from the scene of power in the 1950's as described in Kesey's novel to the scene of power enacted that very day, in the setting of the classroom.

The activities that follow, when carried out without warning, comment, or follow-up over a period of several days, provide a provocative context for the discussion of bio-power operations in *One Flew Over the Cuckoo's Nest*. Together, they constitute the "after" part of a Foucauldian "before and after" picture, a pedagogical strategy for which Foucault is famous and which he uses in *D&P* as an on-going invitation to question, decode, interrogate, hypothesize. Periodically:

> Direct students to stand, take two steps forward, two steps backward, turn completely around twice, touch the toes, and sit.[15]

> Check student attendance. Ask those who are present to supply the names of those who are absent.

> Train a pair of binoculars on a student.

> Raise one finger, silently, as a signal for silence or the start of a class. Keep the finger raised until the class is completely silent.[16]

---

[16]The effectiveness of this disciplinary technique depends on a silence interrupted only by signals: the raised or snapped finger, the clapping of hands, ringing of a bell, or glance from the teacher. Like dogs in obedience classes, students are expected to respond to certain signals automatically, without thought. Ask students to describe signals used by

Invite students to voice complaints or concerns about the course. Take copious notes, copiously. Make sure to record the name of each contributor.

Without warning, dump the contents of a student's backpack on the classroom floor. Give the student a written apology (prepared in advance) and a box of animal crackers; then ask the student to share his/her feelings about the incident with the class.

Ask for a volunteer to deliver a note. While the student waits, write the note; look at the student suspiciously; staple the note in five places; look at the student again, put the stapled note in an envelope and seal the envelope with tape. Hand the note to the student; walk with the student to the door; standing at the door, follow the student with your eyes until he/she is no longer visible.

Write the names of several students on the board. Ask two students to exchange desks.

Ask the students to produce their student identification cards. Walk around the room checking (verifying) each card, looking from the card to the student and vice versa.

While lecturing, help yourself to a pencil or sheet of paper from a student's supply. In the same way, appropriate a student's text to use for the duration of the class or stand directly behind a student and, looking over the student's shoulder, read aloud from his/her text.

While engaged in discussion, walk around the room, straightening several desks or/and the books on several students' desks. Put a kleenex on one of the student's desks.

Look at a student's shoes and ask the student to tell you his/her shoe size. Put a kleenex on one of the student's desks.

As a follow-up, ask students to identify and list parallels between behaviors subject to disciplinary action in the school and in the 1950's psychiatric facility as described in Kesey's novel and using the categories below as a guide, to label the areas of offense: *time* (lateness, absence, interruptions of tasks); *behavior* (impoliteness, disobedience); *speech*

---

various teachers in their own education experience, including those used by college teachers.

(idle chatter, insolence); *body* (irregular gestures, lack of cleanliness); *sexuality* (impurity, indecency).

Identifying Institutional Disciplinary Techniques

Ask students to identify, in *One Flew Over the Cuckoo's Nest*, examples of the following disciplinary techniques:

Surveillance and supervision
Hierarchal assessments and judgments
Coercion[17]
Objectivication and normalization
Transference from deviation to offense[18]
(And techniques of making this transference discreet)

Then, ask the students to investigate (through direct observation, interviews or surreptitious snooping) and to report uses of the above techniques in any institution which imposes controls, e.g., a prison, restaurant chain, school, military group, factory, hospital, retail store, church, family, work site, peer group. (The assignment can be divided and distributed to student groups).

Working in groups or alone, students might then write the *history* of an institutional disciplinary technique. As a pretext, read and discuss the following passage from *One Flew Over the Cuckoo's Nest*:

> You forget—if you don't sit down and make the effort to think back— forget how it was at the old hospital. They didn't have nice places like this on the walls for you to climb into. They didn't have TV or swimming pools or chicken twice a month. They didn't have nothing but walls and chairs, confinement jackets it took you hours of hard work to get out of. They've learned a lot since then …. They've made life look very pleasant with paint and decorations and chrome bathroom fixtures (112).

In *Discipline and Punish*, Foucault invites speculation on the differences between two "penal" scenes: a description of the torture and

---

[17] "The Shock Shop, Mr. McMurphy, is jargon for the EST machine, the Electro Shock Therapy. A device that might be said to do the work of the sleeping pill, the electric chair, *and* the torture rack" (Kesey 64). Students might compare the EST machine and the EMT Team (Educational Management Team) described in Chapter 3.

[18] "If you're a gambler, if they know you to get up a back-room game now and then, all you have to do is spit slantwise and you're a goddammed criminal" (Kesey 25).

death, in 1757, of a would-be regicide and the rules governing the daily lives of prison inmates in 1837. In the same manner, ask students to speculate on the differences between the "old" and "new" "hospital" as described above. Who are the "they" of the passage? What it is 'they" "have learned?"

Another project is to ask students to construct *tool boxes* showing the full range of a single institution's disciplinary apparatuses. As a pretext for this activity, read and discuss the following passage from *One Flew Over the Cuckoo's Nest*:

> ... she's [Nurse Ratched] got that bag full of a thousand parts she aims to use in her duties today—wheels and gears, cogs polished to a hard glitter, tiny pills that gleam like porcelain, needles, forceps, watchmakers pliers, rolls of copper wire ... (Kesey 10)

The bag that looks to the Chief like a "tool box with a hemp handle" (10) is a collection of apparatuses, mechanisms and tools employed in Kesey's asylum to discipline and control patients. Working alone or in groups, using a combination of real-life materials and inventive mock-ups, students can assemble and present "tool boxes" (machines, charts, forms, questionnaires) used currently by one institution (prison, government office, factory, church, hospital, military base) to exclude, reward, credential, invalidate, censor, differentiate, and otherwise "discipline" its employees.[19]

Role-Playing as Patients and Administrators in a "modern" psychiatric facility

Ideally, to investigate current practices and rules in a psychiatric facility, students should enter into it, as patients. Alternatively, students can enact the *scene* of the "asylum," using materials distributed to patients in actual, present day psychiatric facilities. (See Appendix B for the materials, a set of questions and answers from "Mental Health Rights…and Wrongs," a

---

[19] Several of my students have parents who work in United States Government agencies. From interviews with their parents and visits to work-sites, they collected, for their tool boxes, examples and evidence of the following disciplinary apparatuses: performance evaluations, probationary status reports, verbal and written reprimands, cash awards, telephone monitoring, supervisor-controlled agendas, downgradings, reorganizations, job abolitions, parking privileges, training selection, promotions, status designations, e.g., "acting chief"; work assignments, travel approvals; office and room assignments; supplies and equipment allocations.

handbook produced in 1988 by the Maryland Disability Law Center, Inc.[20]) The setting for the activity is an orientation session for new patients. Students role-playing as "patients" should be given the questions and those role-playing as administrators, the answers. The materials provided are a starting point only; "patients" should add their own, "real life" questions and interrogate each response rigorously. Likewise, "administrators" should defend and elaborate on their "answers."

In each of the "answers," patients' rights are spelled out in language that gives the institution broad power to except, exempt, revoke, censor, delay, review, deny, refuse. In some areas of patients' rights, e.g., restraints and medications, the law is precise; in others, e.g., daily activities, it is vague, non-specific, or simply "silent." Although physical punishment and mental abuse (as incarceral techniques) are strictly forbidden, patients are subjected to a system of treatment in which privileges are granted or withheld, depending on the patient's "behavior."

Section 3: The New Historicist Project: New Formulations & Formats

I renounce all my public and private functions! Shame overwhelms me! I cover myself with ashes! I didn't know the date the feeding-bottle was introduced!

— Foucault, *The Confession,* 228

Foucault, as many critics observe, is a lover of facts. His fabled persistence and mania for detail, in fact, mark him as one of the great detectives of all time; yet, little of that *persona* has permeated the new historicist classroom where, despite the change in focus, research is conducted traditionally, by students working in isolation on conventionally conceived term papers.[21] Work conducted in this manner violates the mood of Foucault's approach and inevitably, the meaning of

---

[20] A state agency for the mentally ill created in response to Public Law 99-319, the Protection and Advocacy for Mentally Ill Individuals Act.

[21] Foucault's detached, surgical style has become the mark of new historicist writing; what is absent or suppressed in much of that writing is the sheer exuberance, the vitality and tenacity of Foucault, the man Habermas imagines digging "through archives with the dogged energy of a detective in hot pursuit of evidence" (103); the indefatigable historian who observed, "It is perhaps more difficult to unearth a secret than the unconscious" (*Intellectuals* 214); the compulsive genealogist who, when asked in an interview why he was not writing a genealogy of biopower, replied: "I have no time for that now, but it could be done. In fact, I have to do it" (*On the Genealogy* 232).

the work.[22] Foucault, as Habermas writes, was a detective; his texts are imbued with words and phrases of investigative fervor, e.g., "I wanted to find out," "I wanted to know," "I was looking for." Foucault's energy, moreover, is contagious, even among academics. Wherever "renowned Professors gather'' to discuss Foucault, Bove writes, "there is an air of excitement, energy, and significance that draws one with its promise of pleasure, stimulation, and reward" (vii).

This section argues that Foucault's investigative fervor can be "caught" by students role-playing as detectives or investigative reporters.[23] Research conducted by fictional characters is not frivolous, at least not to a project acutely aware of its own status as fiction. Asked in an interview if he would accept the analysis of his own style as "fictive" in nature and "dramatic" in organization,[24] Foucault replied: "As to the problem of fiction, it seems to me to be a very important one; I am well aware that I have never written anything but fictions" (*The History of Sexuality* 192-193).

In addition to arguing for research approaches that, in Deleuze's words, reclaim "something of the originary critical force of Foucault's work" (*Foucault* viii), this section models the use of new and experimental report formats, projects that show the twists and turns of interrogations and, through a mix of forms and materials (police dossiers, mug shots, maps, pictures, enlarged inserts, forms, personal commentary, statistical tables, architectural drawings, profiles, time tables, indexes, codes), communicate the boldness of Foucault's discourse forays. This

---

[22] The difference of Foucault's projects is in part an effect of the intensity and excitement with which he pursues them. "'Do you imagine,' "Foucault writes, "that I would take so much trouble and so much pleasure in writing, do you think that I would keep so persistently to my task, if I were not preparing—with a rather shaky hand- -a labyrinth into which I can venture ... '?" (*The Archaeology* ... 17).

[23] The power-knowledge connections students are looking for are, after all, secreted; to make them known, students will have to track down, uncover and expose them; like detectives preparing a case, they will, in Foucault's words, have to "produce names" and "point the finger of accusation." (*Intellectuals and Power* 214)

[24] The interviewer, Lucette Finas, provides the following description of Foucault's style: "*The Will to Know* deals with modes of discourse and questions of acts which are themselves caught up in your own discourse, in this order of your discourse which seems rather to be an anti-order. You flit from one point of your argument to another, you engender within your own text discourses that contradict your own, as though the space occupied by your analysis were there in advance and constrained you. Your writing, moreover, strives to depict, before the very eyes of the reader, relations that are abstract and remote" (192).

section also provides a brief overview of the new historicist project, along with some methodological considerations.

Overview & Methodological Considerations

Briefly, the goal of the new historicist project is to investigate the interdependence of history, culture, society, and literature, a formidable task in any stage of an education, let alone the secondary or undergraduate classroom. For students new to the new historicist approach, the project must not be so large as to overwhelm: it might focus on the culture-connections of a single text, one sufficiently removed in time to require an investigation of its cultural and social "facts," perhaps a novel by one of the so-called Lost Generation writers or earlier writers like Wharton, Anderson, Cather, Crane, Chopin, Twain, or Hawthorne. It might also focus on series adolescent literature of the early to middle twentieth century, e.g., Nancy Pembroke, Brenda Starr, Nancy Drew, the Bobbsey Twins, the Motor Girls, depending on students' interests.

Because of the project's emphasis on the analysis of discourse and power relations, the choice of text seems less critical than the choice of issues or time period. The new historicist's goal, after all, is to force the literary text back *into* its time period,[25] to make it play its part in history, to read it as a document that both reflects and *constitutes* the anxieties, issues, concerns of its time. What the cultural anxieties and issues of the novel's time period are, students will learn through the "dig," or research into period archives.[26] Students should know at the start, however, that for the new historicist, the literary text is only one set of discursive practices that constitute a period's discourse.[27]

---

[25] To enact this idea, re-shelve the novel in a section of texts labeled "History." To show how the literary text fights this reclassification, let it fall from the shelf and re-shelve it, forcibly.

[26] See Appendix C for excerpts from literary histories, 1855 to 1926. An analysis of the passages' assumptions regarding the relation of literature to culture increases students' understanding of the new historicist project.

[27] [*Ed.*] Discursive practices are ubiquitous in the human environment and go far beyond the literary text. As emphasized by the philosopher Daniel Dennett (1989), "Our human environment contains not just food and shelter, enemies to fight or flee and conspecifics with whom to mate, but words, words, words. These words are potent elements of our environment that we readily incorporate, ingesting and extruding them, weaving them like spiderwebs into self-protective strings of narrative. Our fundamental tactic of self-protection, self-control, and self-definition is not building dams or spinning webs, but telling stories—and more particularly concocting and controlling the story we tell others—

It is critical to the success of the new historicist project that students are highly motivated and yet, that they understand from the outset the project's difficulties. When asked in an interview how he came upon a certain text, Foucault replied: "By chance, by systematically working through penal reports by medico-legal and psychiatric experts published in professional journals of the nineteenth and twentieth century." The hot-on-the-trail quest for power relations is exciting, but students need to know that as Foucault himself reports, success depends both on systematic investigation and luck or chance, that they may read twenty, thirty, documents from the 1920's and not find one discernable connection between those archives and *The Great Gatsby*, for example, or *The Sun Also Rises*.[28] That is not to say, of course, that the failure to uncover culture-text relations is itself a failure; what is missing or not forthcoming may in itself be noteworthy, e.g., the lack of any reference, in *Huckleberry Finn*, to the Civil War, despite the fact that the novel was written after the war had ended. In any case, students should proceed as though success were imminent, following hunches or following their nose, as the case (in its double meaning) may be.

It has been my experience that students approach the project more confidently and enthusiastically when working *ensemble*, as precinct teams or "search squads." The team provides "a safe place" for students to share anxieties about the assignment and to strengthen their understanding of new historicist theory. As members of a team, students pool talents, share resources and ideas, and widen their research—investigating simultaneously in multiple locations, e.g., biographies, journals, newspapers, letters, interviews.[29] Most important, as "precinct investigators," students may write with impunity against *academe*. With Foucault we might wish educators would expose their own power relations, but as Foucault argues, schools not only do not teach the facts of power; they deny its very connection with knowledge.

---

and ourselves—about who we are." (Dennett, Daniel C. (1989) The Origins of Selves. *Cogito* 3, 163-173).

[28] Power/Knowledge: ... 48.

[29] The team approach also shows the research text, like the so-called "literary text," as an effect of negotiation, exchange, and circulation.

Investigation Procedurals (Appendix D)

To introduce the project and "render visible" certain similarities between the precinct investigation and the new historicist interrogation, I use a "Precinct Investigative Procedures Manual" (see Appendix D), a parody of precinct rules and regulations which sets the mood for—and starts students on—the investigative trail. Through examples drawn from literary texts and the projects of former students, it shows, as clearly as possible, the methods and goals of the historicist project. The handbook also provides examples of new historicism's penchant for detail, its appetite for obscure texts, minutiae, its fascination with power and power-facts, its love of old filing cabinets, its desire to transgress, to breech borders, boundaries, disciplines.

Experimental Project Styles

Conventionally conceived and formatted papers cannot do justice to—or show—what is "passing strange" in the new historicist uncovering. To introduce the issue of presentation, ask students how they might inventively format or display Greenblatt's account of events, in "Towards a Poetics of Culture," of circulation, negotiation, and exchange in the Mailer-Gilmore- Abbot-Adan story (10-11):

> Mailer purchases death-row convict Gary Miller's personal papers.
>
> Mailer uses the papers as a basis for a book, *The Executioner's Song*.
>
> *People* magazine publishes an article on Mailer and the book.
>
> A convict, Jack Abbot, reads the book and establishes a correspondence with Mailer.
>
> Abbot's letters to Mailer are published as a book, *In the Belly of the Beast*.
>
> Abbot is released from prison, kills a man and is returned to prison.
>
> A play about these events, *In the Belly of the Beast*, is written and performed.

In "Towards a Poetics of Culture," Greenblatt calls for critical terms capable of describing the ways in which material moves "from one discursive sphere to another" (11). In the same way that new terms are needed to describe art/culture relations, so new strategies for exhibiting these relations must be devised or formulated. The new historicist project needs a new grammar, a format that shows, and is itself, a mix of discursive and non-discursive materials, that makes visible the relations, in Greenblatt's words, of "entertainment, aesthetics, the public sphere, and private property," e.g., pieces of literary texts, book reviews, advertisements, obituaries, song lyrics, laws, bills, editorials and other cultural flotsam (10). For students, the challenge to display, stage, or exhibit differently is as empowering as the freedom to investigate differently. Although the new presentations will differ, depending on the materials and aims of the project's inquiry, the descriptions below provide a glimpse of what, from my view, a "culture-in-action" project look like.

Willa Cather and *Death Comes for the Archbishop.*

This project is a clunky thick document which includes pictures from popular 1920's journals; recipes from Willa Cather's Kitchen (along with an account of the students actually making and eating Willa Cather's apple pie); reproductions of advertisements from the time period; sections of a student's diary written in New Mexico; a discussion of Cather's novel recorded and faithfully transcribed; mini-sections on Cather's life and times; and experimental headings, e.g., Exploratory Delving, Re-Cap; Back to the Excavation; Unchartered Territory.

Salinger and *Catcher in the Rye.*

This project, shaped as a Book-of-the-Month Club (BMC) paperback, presents Salinger's novel as one of the "goddamn BMC" selections Holden claims to despise and Salinger as one of the club's constituents. The book's back cover carries rave endorsements from Fitzgerald and Hemingway (two BMC writers Holden's brother "just happens" to recommend). The project shows BMC's cultural hegemony through juxtapositionings of BMC titles and accounts of BMC's sales and material transactions. Woven throughout are fragments of *Catcher's* publishing history and reviews, along with copies of the students' letters addressed to Salinger's publishers requesting Salinger's address (unanswered) The effect is to show the BMC as a powerful network that sustains its power by re-publishing it.

In the spring of 1992 (before I "converted" to the team approach) one student took as a project the investigation of Poe's story *The Mystery of Marie Roget.* The project contains many non-traditional materials: personal "to-do" lists; informal progress reports and research "road mappings"; innovative use of fictive reader-responses; quotations from period poems; Library of Congress forms; indexes from 19th century journals; original drawings; citings from current and past studies; original newspaper accounts of Mary Roger's murder; a jig-saw puzzle titled "Who Killed Mary Rogers"? Space precludes reproducing the project in entirety, but the four unedited excerpts below show its spirit and direction.

Samplings From a Student Project: "The Murder of Marie Roget."

From an early progress report:

> I'm so excited for this project .... I haven't finished the story yet, mostly because I have to reread passages after I first read them. I'm very slow reading because it's hard to understand until you read it a second time. The story is about a real murder that took place at this time. The real murder was in New York and the girl's name was Mary Rogers. In my book of Poe, they give where the stories were first published. M.R. first appeared in the *Lady's Companion*, Nov. 1842. Also, throughout the story, Poe mentions newspapers that had reports of the murder. I'm going to go down to the Library of Congress and find the *Lady's Companion* to see what other things were being printed then and also look for those newspapers in the early 1840's and look for the actual accounts of the murder. Poe actually never went to the site of the murder. He wrote his story from the newspaper accounts. I've also looked at three different books about Poe: *Poe, A Collection of Critical Essays*; *Critics on Poe*, and *Poe Poe Poe Poe Poe Poe Poe*. In one of the books I found a time table of his life and a little information on the story. Out of the other two books only one even mentioned the story of M.R. That was in an essay on Poe and the detective story. It said they wouldn't talk about it because it was a real murder. There's another book that I'm getting from another school actually written about the real murder and Poe's story. That should be in the library today. I'm going to the Library of Congress soon and see what I can find. I love this project!

From a later progress report:

> B-CC Library (picture)—POE— (Poe: a Collection of Critical
> Essays)— (critics on Poe)- - (Poe, Poe, Poe, Poe, Poe, Poe, Poe)—
> (POE THE DETECTIVE: The curious circumstances behind the
> mystery of Marie Roget)—Go to Sherwood—Library of Congress.
> Newspaper Room—need dates go to Main Reading Room — search
> Mary Rogers — Poe the Detective (on way from Sherwood) and Who
> Murdered Mary Rogers? —- wait an hour for books—detour to the
> Folger Museum and Theatre—return to Library of Congress—DATES!
> — no time to return to newspaper room have to come back later. — Poe
> the Detective arrives from Sherwood, Who Murdered Mary Rogers from
> Davis Library. Back to L of C w/dates. New York Herald, July 31-Aug
> 31, 1941. Back to see real newspaper. Courier and Enguirer 1841. New
> York Evening Post Jan 10, 1920—run out of time. Come back real
> newspaper had been accidentally sent back, go to microfilm reading
> room to see Lady's Companion run out of time, don't have copy card,
> need to go back.

From a section on the story's publishing history:

> "The Mystery of Marie Roget" was first published in *The Ladies' Home
> Companion*, November, 1842. The story is prefaced by a quotation from
> Von Hardenburg, written in German and translated into English. The
> German version was omitted from the 1943 version. It reappears in
> publications copyrighted after 1965.

From a fabricated reader-response, "Reading a Woman Reading:"

> Imagine if you will, New York City, Monday, the 2nd of August, 1841.
> You are sitting in your kitchen almost fainting from the heat. Your
> favorite newspaper has just arrived, the *New York Courier and
> Enguirer*. The large paper is too wide for you to hold while you read it,
> so you stretch it out on the table in front of you. The first page is full of
> advertisements and information about the stock market. You scan over it
> and turn to the next page which has all the political news from
> Washington D.C., the police and theatrical news of New York City, and
> other tidbits from around the country. You read the police news ....
> another murder, there seem to be a lot of them around these days but
> they all die down pretty quickly. This murder is a young lady, a Miss
> Mary Ann Rogers. Her body was found floating in the Hudson last
> Wednesday afternoon...

From the project's final pages:

> All of Poe's information for his version of Mary's death came from
> newspapers and his imagination. His story comes to no absolute
> conclusion. He leads his story as if to implicate someone. However, just
> when the solution to the murder is expected, there is a note from the
> 'editor' saying that part of the story had been omitted for reasons which
> 'we shall not specify.' It also stated that 'an individual assassin was
> convicted, upon his own confession of the murder of Marie Roget. This
> of course is fictional, because no concrete solution was ever reached in
> the case of Mary Rogers. The 'editor' was none other than E. A. Poe. He
> chose what was and was not published in his story. It is interesting
> though, that Poe named no actual criminal.

The student's project is not a "a paper on Poe" but a well-researched
and creative presentation of culture-in-action. The project draws attention
to the relation of Poe's story to newspaper accounts of the actual murder
and to the facts of the police investigation; it notes that some critics
discuss this relation while others (interestingly) do not; it reveals Poe both
as writer of fiction and fictitious editor of his own writing; it imagines the
"difference" of the story to a woman reading it in New York, in 1841, in a
kitchen so hot she is close to fainting. Finally, the project shows how the
student learns, first hand, that historical work is not conducted in a void
but in real time, with all its constraints and unending small frustrations.

In a follow-up paper analyzing the "difference'' of the new historicist
project, the student writes:

> While researching the murder of Mary Rogers, I was able to read and
> touch an original copy of *The New York Courier and Enguirer*. It was
> incredible to feel the pages of a newspaper that was published at the
> time of the murder; to see what the people of New York City were
> interested in during the 1840's; to laugh at the outrageous remedies
> advertised for outrageous ailments; to read about the death and crime
> that were occurring in the city and elsewhere in the country; to see an
> account of history that was itself actually history.

What a difference between this enthusiastic response to the new
historicist project and the response of students assigned a traditional
"research paper"!

Section 4: Death of the Journal & Other Confessional Writing Practices

> *It seems to me, that all the so-called literature of the self-private diaries,*
> *narratives of the self, etc.—cannot be understood unless it is put in the general*
> *and very rich framework of these practices of the self... What makes the analysis*
> *of the techniques of the self-difficult is two things. First, the techniques of the self-*
> *do not require the same material apparatus as the production of objects, therefore*
> *they are often invisible techniques...*

— Foucault, *On the Genealogy of Ethics*, 250

The anecdote following, a description of an undergraduate class session on *The Scarlet Letter*, is from an article appearing in a 1990 NCTE publication on theory and pedagogy.[30]

> The last day of the unit brought with it one of those 'shining moments'
> Eliot Wigginton describes in the *Foxfire* series. After the students had
> talked about the physical manifestations of Dimmesdale's mental
> anguish, they were asked to respond in their *journals* (emphasis mine) to
> this question: 'Have you (or has someone you know) ever suffered so
> much mental anguish that you became physically ill'? The students
> wrote rapidly for ten minutes. The instructor then asked the students to
> think about a time they had felt the greatest mental anguish as a result of
> an event that had occurred in their lives. She asked the students to
> remember how they felt, and to hold on to that feeling- -and then to
> imagine that this feeling lasted for seven years. The room was
> absolutely quiet. Some students silently wept. 'Now you know how
> Dimmesdale felt', the instructor said, and the class ended" (218).

A "shining moment" in pedagogy—or an appalling abuse of teacher power? Since the advent of reader-response theory, it has been impossible to write with impunity against the use of journals; yet, had I the naked power to change one practice in the classroom, I would displace the journal with the letter. The journal, as analyzed by Foucault, is an apparatus for enforcing self-examination, a vehicle for extracting confession, ...[31] The letter, on the other hand, as Susan Handelman writes

---

[30] Judy Arnold and Benjamin S. Howard, "The Structuralist Community ... "218.

[31] When used as above, the effect can range from despair ("Some students silently wept") to closure and death ("The room was absolutely quiet"). See Foucault's analysis, in "On the "Genealogy of Ethics" (an account of sessions with Michel Foucault, Hubert L. Dreyfus, and Paul Rabinow, at Berkeley in April, 1983), of the journal as a technique of self-

in a letter to me (April 19, 1991) is a tool for "exchange, circulation, and negotiation," a device for opening the class to the freeplay of ideas.[32]

> I totally changed the seminar—asked them [students] to start writing letters to each other and not journals .... I am really glad you pressed me about the journal issue, and told me why you think they don't work. Since they have started writing letters, it has been amazing! Some of them are having a hard time switching, but for the most part, there is this wonderful new openness and exchange of ideas, and it spills over into our oral discussions.

Dear Colleague

November, 1996

If you are among the growing number of teachers who require students to keep journals, I hope in this letter to persuade you to stop. Increasingly, I question our right as teachers to require journals; I think we have no license to compel them, that in assigning them, we sometimes force students into conversations they would not otherwise enter into. By what authority do we ask students to examine their personal responses to literature, to survey the *self?* We are teachers, not priests. Granted, students are free not to confess themselves, but the reality is, writing under the "gaze" and by "habit," they often do. It amazes *me* that having set students up in the confessional, we profess dismay when they divulge!

The uses of journals are not always felicitous. I have personally seen the most egregious breachings of journals by teachers, the sharing of its contents with colleagues, the overstepping of boundaries via comments such as, "Have you thought of seeing a psychiatrist?" or "I admire you for standing up to your father." The abuse of journals is difficult, if not impossible, to establish, but to be fair, haven't we all, at one time or another, made inappropriate use of the journal's margins, e.g., responded to its contents as parents, counselors, psychiatrists, or priests?

Don't you think, too, students are uncomfortable when they know the teacher has read their journals and therefore knows all those "things" which she can publish when she wants to, covertly

---

examination central to the Christian practice of confession. Asked why self-analysis (the keeping of journals, diaries, and so forth) seems "so natural and pleasurable" today, Foucault replied: "It may have been an extremely painful exercise at first and required many cultural valorizations before ending up transformed into a positive activity" (250).

[32] Professor of English, University of Maryland, College Park.

or openly? Reading students' journals increases our power as teachers but at the same time, it takes power away from the students: as journal-readers, we know more about the students than they know about each other. Knowledge is power. Why should we, already in a position of power, be given even more power? And of what value to the class are the journals anyway? The reality is, they are of no value. Journals are private and confidential and we may not, ethically, make use of them in the classroom.

And pity the poor students. Students do not know what a journal is, really. They know a journal is not a diary; they would not write in a journal what they might write in a diary. To the student, the journal is most like a short paper or essay; but precisely to the degree it is not intended to be a formal essay, the journal bewilders students and causes anxiety: "What does she *mean*?" "What does she *want*?" What she "wants" may be to create more openness (or impression of), more freedom (or feeling of), but students know very well that if the journals are evaluated, they, themselves, are *not* free to be open. At this point, the question "what does she want?" takes on real urgency. To the students, it is all very unclear and unfair.

Rather than require students to keep weekly journals (a practice Foucault would abhor) why not ask them to write weekly letters for distribution to the class? Although the distinction between the letter and the journal is, as Derrida points out, not rigorous, the letter is *more* open than the journal and thus *more* subject to play and its corollary, risk. The letter is not unproblematic (*this* letter, for example, is too long by half a mile), but its effects in the classroom (with apologies to Derrida) must be seen to be believed.

Enclosed is a second letter, addressed to students, explaining the use of the letter in the classroom.

___Love,

____Respectfully

____Fondly,

__X__Sincerely,

___Very truly,

Mary Alice Delia

Encl. "Letter to the Class"

Mary Alice Delia

An Open Letter to the Class[33]

November, 1996

Dear Andrew, Betsy, Camillo, Dulce, Effie, Gerry, Harry, Irene, Jack, Klaus, Lenny, Manuel, Natzinga, Ophelia, Peter, Quanz, Richard, Sue, Tamika, U-2, Vi, Werther, X, Yolanda, and Zeke:

Some of you, in other classes, may have been asked to keep journals or other records of your reading experience. In this class, rather than a journal, I would like each of us, for reasons I will make clear, to write a weekly letter and xerox it for class distribution.

The difference between a journal and a letter is that a letter is addressed to a specific person and a journal is not. Although in this case, everyone in the class will read your letter, you should address it to a specific person(s) by name, e.g., another student, a guest lecturer, the entire class, the teacher, an author, a critic, or even a character in a work of fiction. The letter should respond to a specific individual's ideas, attitudes, viewpoints, or feelings, as expressed in essays or narratives read for class assignments, class discussions, or previous letters from students.

In your letter, you may share questions, comments, observations, arguments, suggestions, inspirations, reflections, confusions, frustrations in response to the reading or the issues raised in class. You will find, I believe, that the class letters help make you a better reader, focus your thoughts, raise specific questions for discussion, provide a record of your insights, yield suggestions for paper topics, stimulate discussion and generally help the class become a real community of readers.

Preferably, write your letter immediately after reading the material for that class or after you have read the set of letters from the previous class. Remember to put the date and your name on the letter, as well as the name of the person(s) addressed. Save all your letters in a folder. They may constitute the "raw material" for a final paper, a retrospective essay on "How This Course Has (or Has Not) Changed My Mind."

At the beginning of the semester, I will ask what kind of evaluation you would like these letters to receive. Previous students have stressed the importance of the letter's timeliness. Late letters, like late birthday cards, disappoint everyone and miss the point.

---

[33] For most of the wording in this letter, I am indebted to Susan Handelman.

Section 5: The Letter as Writing and as Discursive Event

> *Letters, Roland discovered, are a form of narrative that envisages no outcome, no closure .... Letters tell no story, because they do not know, from line to line, where they are going.*

— A. S. Byatt, *Possession: A Romance*, 145

No routine, exercise, or assignment in a postmodern classroom escapes analysis, including the displacement of one practice with another. The death of the journal should not go unnoticed and the letter itself should be inquired into, as writing, as a discursive event, and as an assignment imposed on students by a teacher. This section contains activities for helping students read (and tinker with) the letter as *writing*. It also inquires into the letter as a discursive event and offers ideas for exploring its use in an earlier, more visible, culture.

The Letter as Writing

The post card (alphabet, letters, literature, philosophy, text) Derrida writes, "is a kind of open letter (like all letters)" (*The Post Card*: ... 35).[34] To help students comprehend the letter (text) as open, give each a sheet of letter paper and an envelope. Instruct the students to write a letter to the student sitting in front of them (or to the side, as the case may be), and to write the name of the intended receiver on the envelope. When the students have done so, collect the letters and throw them into a MAIL BAG already "stuffed" with an envelope containing an unreadable address, an envelope lacking an address altogether, and an envelope addressed to someone not in the room. Give the mailbag to several students for delivery; when the "dead letters" show up, throw them in the Dead Letter Box (trashcan?) and ask students to theorize what the Dead Letter Box signifies.

As the demonstration is intended to show, despite our desire to guarantee the letter's delivery, not every letter reaches its destination. What the Dead Letter Box helps students "see" is the on-going possibility of an excess or surplus of letters, letters which, if read, might generate

---

[34] See Alan Bass's discussion, in "Translator's Introduction" to *The Post Card*: ..., of Derrida's play on *poste* (xxvii).

new meanings or challenge the "received" meaning of letters already "addressed." Like writing, *ecriture*, inscription, the meaning of the letter is not reducible to the letter; the meaning of the letter is a function of the system which puts it into play.

The Dead Letter Contest

As a playful introduction to Derrida's argument that the "dead letter" is the letter which guarantees the letter (the postal system),[35]construct and display in class a DEAD LETTER BOX, e.g., an old mailbox or shoe box painted red or black, with the words "Dead Letter Box" imprinted on its side. Hold a "Dead Letter Contest'' for the best Dead Letter dropped into the box. Prizes should be thematized, e.g., a letter opener, a boxed set of note cards or envelopes, a stamp, change of address cards.

The Dead Parcel Auction

Distribute Derrida's transcription, in *Post Card*, of a "barely erased" inscription on a wall in Charlottesville, Virginia, detailing the operations of the Dead Letter Office" (124). According to Derrida's transcription, letters "without assignable addresses" are destroyed, but *dead parcels* are sold at auction. Following the "Dead Letter Contest," ask students to construct "dead parcels" for auction. Use the proceeds to purchase pizzas.[36]

---

[35] See Derrida's proposition, in "The Purveyor of Truth," that "a letter can always not arrive at its destination" (187). For Derrida, it is the "dead letter" that guarantees the structure of the postal system. As Alan Bass, translator, notes: "For Derrida, writing is always that which is an excess remainder, *un reste*." In French, Bass explains, "mail delivered to a post office box is called *poste restante*, making the dead letter office the ultimate *poste restante*, literally, 'remaining mail.' "Without the possibility that a letter "can always *remain* in the dead letter office," Bass explains, "there would be no delivery of letters to any address at all" (207).

[36] For other playful ideas, read Derrida' s interrogations of the "Dead Letter Office" in *Post Card*, pp. 124-125. How might one enact in class, for example, Derrida's words: "I am sending it [the letter] to you to ask you to rip it up and to throw it in little pieces out of the window of your car, going fast ...?" (125)

Taking Pen in Hand

> *... as to ... the graphic 'code', considered not from the point of view of the intention of signification or of denotation, but of style and connotation; problems of the articulation of graphic forms and of diverse substances, or the diverse forms of graphic substances (materials: wood, wax, skin, stone, ink, metal, vegetable) or instruments (point, brush, etc. etc.); ...*

— Derrida, *Of Grammatology*, 87

Writing, in most classrooms, gets the short end of the grammatological stick. As Ulmer might complain: We are willing to read anything students write, provided it is typed, doublespaced, and presented to us on standard-size paper. Rather than take the limited (and boring) view of writing as word-processing, we should show students writing as a discourse constituted by "style and connotation" rather than "signification" and "denotation." Graphology, or writing, makes use of multiple materials, instruments, and styles, all of which, if given opportunities, students can make playful use of.

The most engaging letters, in my experience, are inscribed in ink, a formidable process as those who have dipped pen-in-inkwell well know. Quills, inkwells, and ink are not difficult to procure but to produce an even flow of ink is an art requiring much practice. "Pupils will learn by experiment," the 1882 *Colliers* advises, "that if they raise the pen from the ink suddenly, it will be too full, and apt to blot; if very slowly, the attraction of the fluid will leave none in the pen; and therefore, a moderate motion must be used. *One experiment is worth hours of talking*" (Emphasis mine).[37]

Writing devices and paraphernalia fascinate students. I have, and use in class, an old writing desk, of the type fancied by antique collectors. The desk, and its secret compartments, so intrigues students that several have designed and constructed their own, replete with supplies. Beyond desks and inkwells are scrolls, scriptoriums, manuscript illumination, engraving, carving, skywriting, braille, chalks, colored inks, signets, seals,

---

[37] *Colliers'* advice continues, in words of interest to students of Foucault: "Attention to this will save many a blot. Cleanliness is as absolutely necessary for the well-being of the pen as for our own."

ideographics, and a host of other forms, substances, and procedures that introduced in the classroom, stimulate interest in writing as *writing*.

Deconstructing the Public/Private Opposition

> *He [Epicurus] obviously already had some difficulty distinguishing between private and public letters: ...*
>
> — Derrida, *Post Card,* 91

Write a dictionary definition of the word *letter* on the board, e.g., "a written or printed message intended for the perusal only of the person or organization to whom it is addressed." Webster's words to the contrary, letters, some letters, although addressed to specific individuals, go, as Derrida observes "beyond the limits of a letter" to reach "the proportions of a discourse" (*Post Card* 91). Divide students in groups and give each group one of the letter types listed below. (Students themselves might prepare models.) Ask each group to determine the degree to which the letter type they are given is, by definition, a *letter*, and then to share their determinations with the class.

Scented letters
Round robin or chain letters
Personalized form letters
Second- or third-class letters
Letters to the editor
Open letter
Dear Santa letters
Letter cards (post cards)
Faxed letters
Lettergrams
Telegrams
Certified letters

Alternatively, distribute the entire list of letters to each group for distribution on a public/private continuum. Display the distributions on the board for comparison and discussion.

The Letter as Discourse

> *Therefore beware, and be even over-cautious, rather than not cautious*
> *enough, for a letter may serve as a sure witness in cases where you might never*
> *suppose it could be used. It may live and bear testimony for years—it does not*
> *change with time or circumstance—it is a warrantee deed of whose responsibility*
> *you can never be free.*

> — *Manners, Culture, and Dress,* 1881

The same letter Derrida interrogates as writing, Foucault investigates as discourse.[38] Following Foucault's methodology (as described earlier), students should commence interrogation of the letter by identifying its current modes of existence and by analyzing its power relations in present-day culture. A quick trip to a card shop shows the letter's connectedness to virtually all areas of late twentieth century culture.

> *Social & Cultural*: Invitations, Birthdays, Anniversaries, Births, Religious Holidays, Mother's Day, Father's Day, Grandparents' Day, Retirement, Deaths, Valentine's Day, Illness, Divorce, Graduations, Marriages, Thanksgiving, Apologies, Commemoration, Appreciation, Change of Address, promotion.
> *Business, Church, Law*: Letter of credit, testimony, appointment, *marque*, advice, introduction, attorney, delegation, intent, testamentary, credentials, patent, absolution, administration, request, credence, notification, authorization, resignation, application, recommendation, acceptance, rejection.

Extracting the Letter's Elements

To suggest how to approach the investigation of the letter as discursive event, give each student a lemon and hold a "lemonsqueezing" contest (with a prize going to the student who extracts the most juice). Explain that in the same way they squeezed the lemons, Foucault "pressures" the event, extracting knowledge first, of its elements and then, of its participation in other discursive practices. Then, hold a "letter-squeezing" contest, with a prize going to the student who extracts from the letter, the most elements. Letter elements include (but are not limited to):

---

[38] For a helpful discussion of the term *discourse*, see Paul A. Bove's "Discourse" in *Critical Terms for Literary Study*, ed. Frank Lentricchia and Thomas McLaughlin (Chicago: U of CP, 1990): 50-65.

Letter Elements: notaries, seals, stamps, witnesses, mail classifications, complimentary closings, titles, addresses, enclosures, signatures, ernbossments, colors, sizes, postmasters, postal workers, scanners, post offices, carbons, blind copies, fax machines, mail boxes, imprints, prepared stamps, stamped mail, weights, rates, routes, deliveries, pick-up hours, placement and classification of mail boxes, inter-office mail routes, postal practices.

Finding the Letter's Discourse Rules

If students look at the letter through the eyes of Foucault, they will see the mail box, like the confessional box, as a component of twentieth-century power relations. What they will not see as clearly, however, are the rules which organize and govern the letter and constitute it as discourse. To find those rules, they will have to trace the letter back to a period when the rules were published, to the late nineteenth century collections of letter-writing guides, e. g., *Manners, Culture, and Dress* (1881).[39]

MANNERS
Culture and Dress
of the
Best American Society,

including

Social, Commercial and Legal Forms
Letter Writing, Invitations, & also valuable
suggestions on Self Culture and
Home Training

Nowhere in culture are the rules and regulations governing the production of letters more visible than in the cultural compendiums of the late nineteenth century. Publications like *Manners, Culture, and Dress* (and others) expose the letter's pervasiveness in nineteenth century society and culture:[40] they also show that the language regulating the

---

[39] As a tool for writing the history of current American cultural practices, *Manners, Culture, and Dress* is invaluable. Now out of print, the book should be re-published and made available to students in introductory "American literature" classes.

[40] "Every position in life demands letter-writing," writes the editor of the 1882 *Colliers Cyclopedia*. Here is a small sampling of social situations that dictated the letter: Introducing a sister to a Schoolmate; Introducing a Gentleman to a Lady Friend; To the Father of a Young Lady, Asking Her Hand in Marriage; A Gentleman, After Meeting a Lady at a Party, Asking Permission To Pay His Addresses; A Gentleman Asking His

writing of letters is permeated with language governing behavior in all areas of culture. The letter, for the late nineteenth century, is the great junction house of language, the place where discourse from all areas of culture circulates and redistributes its effects as power. Below, from *Manners, Culture, and Dress*, are statements showing the letter's power to *dictate*:

> That we are a nation of poor writers is attributable more to carelessness (shall we say laziness?) than to any other one thing.
>
> Every boy and every girl may and ought to learn to write well. The habit, like all good habits, should be formed in youth and when once formed is formed for life.
> Avoid monograms, floral decorations and landscapes. Unless of an elaborate and costly design they have an appearance of cheapness, and are decidedly in bad taste.
>
> The excellences of a nicely written letter are embraced in one word, *neatness*. All blots, erasures, interlinings, will never be seen in a neat letter.
>
> If your correspondent be a person of culture, he will certainly notice any errors in your epistle. You cannot afford to be thought either ignorant or careless.
>
> In closing a letter, the degrees of formality are shown as follows: 'Yours truly', 'Truly yours', 'Very truly yours', 'Yours very truly', 'Sincerely yours', 'Cordially yours', 'Respectfully yours', 'Faithfully yours', 'Affectionately yours', 'Lovingly yours.'"
>
> Letters of business need attention in a work of this kind, because they are those most frequently to be written .... Let the style be marked by the utmost directness; use no flowers of speech, no metaphor, no rhetorical graces; they are out of place. Use plain Saxon English .... An elaborate or illegible signature intended to make an impression on the beholder is exceedingly snobbish.

Students may well argue the "ridiculousness" of the rules governing the production of letters in nineteenth century culture; in response, the new historicist teacher will point out that it is precisely in the

---

Betrothed to Name the Day; Complaints of a Lady's Coolness; Explaining an Apparent Slight; Complaining of Not Receiving a Letter.

"ridiculousness" of the letters, the "passing strangeness" of their language, that we see the hierarchical structures, social constraints, and disciplinary mechanisms underlying the production of letters in our own late twentieth-century culture.

In a 1976 lecture delivered to his students, Foucault expresses frustration with the failure of his research "to develop into any continuous or coherent whole" ("Two Lectures..." 78). I am well aware that the same complaint could be lodged against this chapter and the one before, for the failure to develop "a continuous" or "coherent" program for a new historicist pedagogy. However, like Foucault, I would argue that the ideas presented in these chapters are "merely lines laid down for you to pursue or to divert elsewhere, for me to extend upon or re-design as the case might be'' (78-79).

CHAPTER FIVE
The Propshop

*... the **word** and the **thing** affect people differently.*

— Gregory L. Ulmer, *Applied Grammatology...*, 264

Recently, I was invited to give a one-hour presentation on the implications of postmodern theory for the teaching of poetry to a group of twenty secondary English teachers, most of whom knew very little about the ideas of Derrida or Foucault. The assignment was formidable. Although theoretically a postmodern practice cannot be prefaced or understood in advance of its own performance, what *occurs* in a postmodern practice is the effect of philosophical positionings that require much study. These positionings, to borrow Susan R. Horton's succinct formulation, hold that interpretation is arbitrary; meaning, contingent; truth, inaccessible, and intention, irretrievable (278). Such radical new ideas cannot be gotten into a nutshell and even if they could, a nutshell or lecture approach is *not* good postmodern pedagogy!

As Ulmer argues and this chapter contends, a practice true to the values and methods of new theory will, among other things, make use of "objects" as well as "words"[1]; it will employ props, models, objects, and apparatuses to interrogate theory's ideas and concepts. In the workshop, I wanted to show the postmodern concept of meaning as an outcome of a theory of meaning and not, as new criticism would have it, as a truth fixed in the stars. To that end, I put together a propshop, the inventory of which was as follows:

academic gown and hood
twenty jigsaw puzzles (all white, found in toy stores)
grade book
cotton balls
extension cord

---

[1] [*Ed.*] Despite the seeming opposition between words and objects in this sentence, the book is actually inspired by the idea of a sort of continuity between them, as words can be considered as a specific type of objects. Not only they have material features (in both their spoken and written forms) but, as shown by many methodological excercises in this book, they can also provide the same type of pedagogical support offered by concrete objects. The opposition between words and objects is only superficial and functional here to the description of how the workshop has been conducted.

3 × 5 card
magnifying glass
stop watch
the text of a poem

The Workshop

Arriving early at the workshop, I placed, on each desk, the disassembled pieces of a small, all-white jigsaw puzzle. At the appointed hour, I positioned myself at the lectern and adopting a professorial air, waved the entering teachers to their seats. "Welcome to the workshop!" I said. "Please put all books, notebooks, and legal pads under your desks. In this workshop there will be no lecture and no note-taking; all the activities are experiential."

With great ceremony, I then donned the academic gown and hood. "Bear with me," I said. "What my costume is supposed to suggest is the scene of teacher authority. In this scene, I will play the pedagogue, the one "presumed to know" and you, if willing, will role-play as undergraduates."

"Today's lesson is on poetry. The puzzle pieces on your desks are intended to represent the parts of a poem. As students, your task is to fit the parts together into a meaningful whole. For this assignment," I announced, setting the stop watch, "you have precisely two minutes."

The teachers fell immediately to work. While they puzzled, I circled the room officiously, checking the students' progress, making notations in the gradebook, and pelting some of the students (from behind) with cotton balls. At the end of two minutes, I yelled "STOP"! Those who have completed the puzzle will receive an *A*. All others fail."

Cries of outrage mixed with catcalls filled the air. "What???" "This is ridiculous!" "I didn't have enough time!" "No one could do this." "I can't do puzzles without pictures."

"Listen to the excuses!" I said. "As your 'teacher', I assure you the fault is not in the poem, but in yourselves; that as readers, you are incompetent."

The participators protested. "A puzzle is not a poem," one teacher challenged. "What was the point of this activity?"

To signify a move "outside" the classroom, I removed the academic gown and spoke less authoritatively. "The point was for you to feel what students experience when we ask them to explicate or find the "meaning" of a poem they have never seen. How *did* you feel? Can you describe your emotions?"

"I was nervous," one teacher volunteered. "Look—my hands are *still* shaking! I can't believe I let myself get that upset." "I was afraid everyone would finish except me," another said. "I felt anxious and self-conscious."

"Why were you hitting us with cotton balls?"

"Why didn't you complain?" I asked.

"To whom?" the teachers asked. "We didn't know what was going on."

"The cotton balls are part of the 'act'," I said. "They are meant to show the violence of the assignment, the scene of cognitive terrorism. The anxieties you have just described are the same students experience when asked to "puzzle out" a poem. To students, the poem *is* a puzzle; the words or puzzle pieces 'mean' only in relation to a picture the students have no knowledge of."

"But a poem has words," one teacher objected. "The problem is students don't know how to *read*."

"They can read," another added, "but they don't read *closely*."

"By reading closely," I asked, squinting into the text of a poem through the lens of a magnifying class, "do you mean like this?"

The teachers laughed. One, however, seemed (and perhaps rightly so) more exasperated than amused. "I think we all know what it means to read a poem closely."

"Yes and no," I hedged. "We know how to read closely (and cleverly) enough to *make* the poem mean. From our own teachers, we have learned techniques for *making* a poem mean. But the students don't understand meaning as an effect of a *theory* of meaning; they think meaning is something inherent in, hidden in the poem.

"Are you saying there *is* no meaning in the poem, that we are free to read it just 'any which way'?"

It is precisely here, however, in moments of radical epistemological challenge, that play can rescue what otherwise is surely lost. Taking literally the teacher's idea of reading 'any which way', I turned Frost's poem upside down and sideways, twisting and stretching my head in order to read it. "As you see," I said, "the poem *can* be read 'any which way.' The teachers chuckled politely.

"A poem," I continued, "is not a lottery ticket. Its 'meaning' is nothing one can scratch and uncover." I rubbed the text of the poem with the edge of a dime (not exactly Barthe's idea of bliss) and buffeted by play, the teachers played along.

"Here," one said, "try a quarter!" More laughter.

"The point is," I said, "meaning is nothing that can be shaken out of a text." I rattled the text with one hand and with the other, let fall to the floor a 3 x 5 card on which I had written the word *MEANING*. "Ooops!" I said, retrieving the card. "I was saving this for an emergency!"

"What postmodernism maintains," I went on, "is that meaning is a function not of "the poem" but of a *theory* of the poem. To generate meaning, in other words, we have to plug the text into a *theory* of meaning."

As this point, I taped the poem to one end of an extension cord and surveyed the room. "This room has four outlets," I announced. "Imagine each outlet as a meaning-generator. The outlet on the far wall we can designate as the New Critical outlet. It will produce the paradoxes, ambiguities, qualifications and ironies that show the poem as a puzzle."

"What about this one, over here?"

Thanks to the propshop, the teachers' interest in theory is sparked and at the end of the session, several teachers remained to talk and to ask for reading suggestions. The point is not to re-play the entire workshop but to show the power of props to open the classroom (at all levels) by putting theory's issues (whatever they may be) into play. A propshop, properly speaking, is a *property* shop, a collection of objects which show, translate, and transmit the *properties* of theory in ways that demystify it and make it understandable. The first task of the teacher, after all, is to explain herself, and as Joseph Beuys has said, "If you want to explain yourself, you must present something tangible"; you must translate thought into action and action into object" (245).

For the idea of the propshop, I am indebted to Gregory Ulmer's work on the performance art of Joseph Beuys, professor of sculpture at the Academy of Art in Dusseldorf. In the avantgarde art of Beuys, as Ulmer analyzes it, the object or model which Derrida writes of theoretically (229) is produced literally (250) as an object which embodies the idea and shows its motivation. The postcard, for example, which Derrida evokes as a theoretical model in a text, Beuys produces literally as an object that signifies "the phenomenon of 'transmitting' as such" (250). One the role of models and objects in pedagogy, Beuys is explicit:

> The physicist can think about the theory of atoms or about physical theory in general. But to advance his theories he has to build models, tangible systems. He too has to transfer his thought into action, and the action into an object. I am not a teacher who tells his students only to think. I say act; do something; ..." (*AP* 245).

Beyond their value as objects which embody and show theory, props invite students to enter into theory, to *act*, to take playfully theory's invitation to perform. At the 1992 MLA National Convention, I presented a paper arguing the need for a more playful postmodern practice. The presentation was laced with concrete suggestions and demonstrations. To show the "soft touch" of what Bourdieu calls symbolic violence, for example, I pelted my audience with handfuls of giant-sized cotton balls. To my delight, the cotton balls returned! I then threw *rocks* (soft spongy ones, to be sure). These too, returned, along with whoops of laughter, an outpouring of questions, and a general breakdown in academic decorum. The invitation to play is not a preface. The inviter cannot know in advance how her summons will be received or how she, herself, will respond to the response.

Shortly, I will open the propshop that has taken eight years to assemble and without which, I cannot now imagine teaching certain concepts or points in theory. Please do not expect anything fabulous. The props themselves are not patented; most are simple, ordinary objects of the sort one finds in the house or workshop, e.g., a piece of wire, a mirror, a salt shaker. Other props come from the toy store which, when looked at long enough through the lens of theory, transforms to a postmodern playshop. About play, toys themselves seem to know nothing: there is nothing indeterminate, indecisive or ambiguous about a yellow rubber duck! Yet, as an actor in a postmodern theatre, the duck, as I will show, is superb.

Still other props come from the classroom itself, from what Ulmer, writing of Beuys' work, calls "the fundamental apparatuses of the school... — blackboards, chalk, erasers, desks, pointers, lectures—..." (*AG* 247). In a postmodern classroom, these "fundamental apparatuses" — if one remains alert to possibilities – can function as devices for introducing complex theoretical concepts. An example makes my point.

One day, as I was hastily erasing old notes from the blackboard in order to write new ones, a student called out in alarm: "Oh, no! Not another Miss Lanaham! "

"Who is Miss Lanaham?", I asked, not turning around.

"Our eighth-grade teacher. She never completely erased the board," the student explained. "We used to get headaches trying to read her writing."

I stepped back and looked at my own sloppily erased blackboard. Imprinted in the heavy chalk dust in which I had just written were bits and pieces of letters, characters lopped off at the top, vestiges and tracings of earlier writing.

"Well, this is interesting!" I said excitedly. "What you are looking at, is a concrete representation of Derrida's concept of the *trace*."

"Huh?"

"For Derrida, all writing retains the trace, the sign or mark of the presence of past writing. Look at the writing on the board carefully; don't look for the 'meaning' of the words; just look at the writing *as* writing. If you can do that, you will see that in the new writing is neither the complete presence or complete absence of the old writing, but its *trace*, right?"

"Yes. Get rid of it."

"O.K." With a wet paper towel, I wiped the board until no trace, no writing, was visible. "Is this better?" I asked.

"Much better," the student replied. "Now I can't see the old writing."

I wrote the student's words on the board then erased the word *old*:

"Now I can't see the *writing*."

"Precisely Derrida's point," I said. "We don't want to see writing as writing; we want to look right through it to see meaning. Writing inscribed on a newly washed board is easier to see through and that's how we wrongly think of writing—as a clear glass to look through quickly in order to get at the really important stuff ... the writer's 'truth' or 'meaning.'"

"But the whole point is to write clearly," the students objected, "so others can understand you."

"But writing, as this scene on the blackboard shows, is *not* 'clear.' Writing is not wired or linked to anything but itself and as itself, it alludes to nothing but writing. Washing the board does not wash away the fact that language is sticky stuff, that part of the old always inhabits or loops through the new. Writing on a clean board does not guarantee a clean or "clear" meaning (although we want to think so.) Regardless of how well we wash the board, the 'meaning' of our words is never clear; each word we write is trouble; each translates infinitely, moves from one meaning in one context to other meanings elsewhere."

"This is pretty heavy stuff," one student protested.

"*Au contraire*. It's precisely the 'heaviness' of meaning that Derrida questions."

Chalk *chalk* up as a prop (settle a score/walk a chalk line). And erasers (*erasurers*/dustbusters/ghostbusters.) Often one need go no further than the most minimally furnished college classroom for object-lessons in theory. "It is not just that the familiar or banal objects (whether from the classroom or other areas of life) are charged with significance by becoming part of an art Action but that they *already* carry charges of energy" (*AP* 247), Ulmer writes. In the same way that Derrida teaches us to look closely at language, we can train ourselves, in the classroom, to look closely at *things*.

A List of Props (The prop shop alphabet)

Below are the gizmos, tools, gadgets, machines, toys, objects, and apparatuses that constitute this chapter's propshop along with anecdotal suggestions for putting them into play. While many of the props were developed in the high school classroom, they (or others) are appropriate in the undergraduate classroom or in any classroom where theory is taught, regardless of student age or course level. In the rigorous work of teaching and learning theory, props can play a critical role. They help to explain theory's operations by making them more visible; they also introduce theory more "postmodernally" by opening the text of the classroom to play.

Some of the props, activities, and scenes that follow are discussed within a briefly described curricular context; others are not. The goal of this chapter is not to show how props fit into a pre-determined curriculum, but to argue the on-going value of props in a performative, postmodern practice. Obviously, students at all levels will need follow-up reading assignments and time in class to discuss the implications of the props and demonstrations.

To suggest how the props *might* work in a curricular context, I have indicated, for each prop, an aspect, term, element, or concept in theory which it signifies, embodies or can be made to interrogate. I realize the propshop assumes a knowledge of theory that some readers may not yet have, but I do not think a lack of familiarity with theory will prevent the reader from understanding the propshop's emphasis on play. For lack of a better idea, I list the props in alphabetical order. The propshop alphabet itself is not full. It has no E, I, K, L, N, O, Q, U, W, X, Y, Z.

ACADEMIC ROBE {the scene of academe}

More than any other prop, the academic robe, when donned in the classroom, shows students the *mise en scene* of pedagogy, the appeal to professorial credentialing and power. The robe itself can be worn playfully: it can be embellished with campaign buttons, stickers, rhinestone pins, or accompanied by a long double strand of inexpensive pink pearls and feathered hat. To show the mix of discourses which constitute the language of pedagogy, add a crucifix and an army hat.

ALPHABET BLOCKS {the prison house of language}

A child's wagon filled with alphabet blocks can help students comprehend the idea of language as a "prison house." The idea for this prop (as for others) was born of sheer frustration. I had been trying, without success, to explain Derrida's idea that language cannot be critiqued from without, that one cannot "get out" of language in order to see or comprehend its "truth" or "reality;" that language itself is a prison house.

"Language," the students righteously declared, "is not a prison house. Language does not close doors; it *opens* them."

In response, I stood a student in a trash can. "Look," I said, "a student in a trashcan. We know the student is in a trash can because from where we sit, we can *see* the trash can. The world, after all, is bigger than a trash can. But how do we know the world itself is not a trash can? How can we "get out of the trashcan" to see?"

"Easy!" the students replied. "Just step out!" The next day, I brought in the wagon and blocks and, to put the alphabet on view, pulled the wagon several times around the room and then dumped the blocks on the floor. "See how many words you can make of these blocks in one minute," I said. In short order, the students produced three or four short words, using up most of the blocks.

"This is pretty juvenile" one student complained.

"Put that in writing," I said. "Use the blocks."

"We need more blocks."

"There are no more or 'other' blocks," I said. "To criticize this assignment, you will have to deconstruct your 'words' and re-use the letters to form new words. There is no way to write against blocks without using blocks. In the same way, there is no way to write against words without using words. If you think of the blocks as language, then you will understand postmodern theory's idea of language as a prison house. There's no back door, no fire exit. The only way out is to go back in."

"This is stupid!" one student exclaimed. "It doesn't prove *any*thing!" She picked up a block and hurled it across the floor.

APRON {gender issues}

A kitchen apron opens a text quickly to issues of gender. The speaker in Arnold's "Dover Beach," for example, is generally assumed to be male. When the lines "Come to the window, sweet is the night air!" are read by or delivered to a woman wearing an apron, however, the lyric situation is radically recontextualized. Because the woman-in-apron is reductive, the prop should be used carefully; but especially in the reading of "Dover Beach," the apron deconstructs a certain "grand male melancholia" from which as a woman, I have personally always felt excluded.

BALANCE SCALE {the weighted word}

An inexpensive (flea market) balance scale helps students understand the role of culture in determining a word's value or weight. To demonstrate, write "Doe" on one 3 x 5 card and "Roe" on another. Put one card in each balance tray. Students will see the scale balances; the name cards are equal in weight. Add the word "John" to the "Doe" card and "Mary" to the Roe card. To *show* the greater cultural weight attached to the male name, tip the scale in its favor. Ask students to account for the privileging of the male name, e.g., in marriage. They will be quick to suggest that the greater weight of the man's name is determined by societal and/or cultural values customs and norms.

This demonstration may strike the reader as simplistic, but in fact, it opened eyes and minds in my classroom even if it did not immediately produce changes in positions. The idea for the scale came from a class discussion during which a seventeen-year-old male, announced: "You better believe if I get married, my wife is going to take my name!"

I am not certain of my exact reply, but I do know it contained the word *weigh* ... possibly, "Why should your name weigh more than hers?"

"I don't know. It just does," he said.

The idea of a name's *weight* stuck with me. I bought the balance scale, brought it class, and carried out the demonstration described above. I then asked the student: "Do you still claim your name *weighs* more?" He laughed. "O.K. You got me. I guess it's my culture. But she is still going to take my name!"

Other uses of the scale include the balancing of comparably sized books, e.g, paperback copies of *Portrait of the Artist as a Young Man and Their Eyes Were Watching God*.

COMPASS {the center and freeplay}

A twin compass and the text of Donne's "A Valediction: Forbidding Mourning" can help students understand Derrida's idea of a center which both opens and closes play. In Donne's famous conceit, the "fixed foot" of the woman functions as a center which both allows (opens) and limits (closes) the lover's play. Although the lover "far doth roam," he is, of necessity, never far from the controlling center. In a feminist reading, the woman's movements can be seen as a function of her lover's trajectory; as the "fixed foot," she moves only "if th' other do" or not at all. As a "pure foot," the woman is doubly "fixed" or nailed: once by her lover's desire and again, by Plato.

Two students, a male and a female, can enact the drama of Donne's text. The female plants her feet firmly on the floor; the lovers join right hands; when the male's feet roam in an arc, the female is forced to lean after him. Rather than "hearken" after the "circling" male, however, today's female is apt to let him fly!

Frost's sonnet, "A Silken Tent," can also be used to introduce the idea of a center that is both free and not free to play.

COTTON BALLS {symbolic violence}

A student pelted with cotton balls will not complain; cotton does not tear the flesh. The effects, however, as Bourdieu argues, are *felt*; the pelting shows Bourdieu's concept of symbolic violence, the soft brutality of the unspoken rules and practices in any field of play (*Distinction* 511): the obligatory contribution at the office; the box of Girl Scout cookies dutifully purchased from "the boss"; Lear's request for the measure of his daughters' love. The softness of the cotton balls emphasizes the nature of the violence, the violation one senses, feels, but dares not acknowledge.

DISAPPEARING INK {occulting in the binary}

Disappearing ink makes visible the occulting of a term in a binary opposition. Write the dichotomy *mind/body* on a sheet of paper, but write the word *mind* in regular ink and the word *body* in disappearing ink. As the word *body* disappears, ask the students to theorize the disappearance of the "body" from the scene of pedagogy. Repeat the procedure with the dichotomy *male/female*. Ask students to account for the fading of women's voices in the very classroom in which they sit.

FISHING POLE {the Socratic dialogue}

A fishing pole playfully brings to surface the scene of the Socratic dialogue. In the classroom, we respond to questions with questions and like Socrates, we think our questions quite playful but as Barthes writes, this thinking is one of our many illusions. We use our questions like fishing poles to bait students but on the topic of what Barthes calls "the real game," the game of *fishing* itself, we are silent. And the effect of our questions, like that of Socrates' *play*, Barthes writes, is to make the subject "more stable than ever." (*Roland Barthes* 142)

When I sit on the edge of a desk, fishing pole in hand, I show the pedagogical desire to *catch* something, e.g., a certain response, a confession, a change of attitude or position.

GALLOWS {the death of play}

A working gallows (constructed from scrap lumber) functions in the classroom as a *raised frame*, a playful device for exhibiting violence and the suspension or death of play, e.g., Snoopy or Raggedy Ann hung by a foot. A hung book shows the Barthesian concept of the death of the Author. What the scaffold puts out of play is simultaneously put *into* play: the loss of play is seen and experienced as visceral.

In the new historicist classroom, the gallows is a powerful enactment of the disciplinary apparatus Foucault finds at the heart of the great institutions of "human science." Deconstructed (literally), the gallows has other prop values: for Mary Shelley's *Frankenstein*, the base serves as a table for Victor's base experiments and the gallows post, made of sturdy oak, serves as a post office, a location for publishing various and assorted texts: personals, advertisements, graffiti, announcements, newspaper clippings.

The gallows is also useful for introducing Kristeva's argument that the sacred murder contains violence by confining it to a single place where it signifies the symbolic order (*Revolution* 75).

GROUNDING WIRE {the appeal to foundations}

A wire run between two books shows the grounding of one in the other. In Salinger's *Catcher in the Rye*, for example, Holden Caulfield claims to be "put off" by people who sound and act "phony"; a wire run from the *Catcher* to Plato's *Republic* shows Holden's appeal to platonism and the idea of that which is "genuine" or "true." In New Critical classrooms more interested in irony than in Holden's subversive attack on middle class values, Holden is identified as the biggest "phony" in the book. A wire run from *that* proposition to Plato, shows it no less grounded than Holden's. A short piece of grounding wire has more power (in the classroom) than a pocket knife (though the knife too has its uses).

HATS {ventriloquism}

Hats help students respond to texts more playfully. My own repertoire includes hardhats, tams, motorcycle helmets, military hats, top hats, baseball hats, bandannas, and especially, hats with veils. Hats bring cultural differences and values into play. Different hats can be distributed to students who, as "interpreters" for the social, cultural, or occupational groups signified, must speak for and represent those groups vigorously. Each hat provides a different perspective and some contain their own material critiques: hardhats and helmets are cumbersome and impair hearing; veils limit, blur, distort; top hats are topheavy. In workshops, I myself often wear a hardhat to show that the deconstructive operation is not without risk. Opening the text to the freeplay of signifiers is like drinking from an unlabeled bottle: the effects cannot be guaranteed.

JOKER {the floating signifier}

"Sly, slippery, and masked, an intriguer and a card, like Hermes, he is neither king nor jack, but rather a sort of *joker*, a floating signifier, a wild card, one who puts play into play" (*Dissemination* 93). For Derrida, the joker signifies writing; distributed as a wild card in class, the joker permits the student who has it subversively to displace or supplement the topic/issue at hand with another, one of the student's choosing. During a class discussion of Tennyson's "Ulysses," for example, a male student with a wild card played it as a *question*: "What do you think about girls who date older men?" A classroom, even a grammatological classroom, is a stacked deck which the joker playfully redistributes—as a new game, to be sure—but a game which, according to Derrida, ensures new life as well as death.

LEGO BLOCKS {bricolage}

In the same way that the alphabet blocks help students comprehend language as a prison house, a set of lego (logo) blocks helps students understand *bricolage* as the attack on structure from within or the art of building "castles with debris" (*OG* 139). To start the demonstration, divide the class in three groups. Give the first group the lego blocks and five minutes to construct a wagon. Give the second group five minutes to deconstruct and reassemble the wagon as a Model-T; and the third group, five minutes to engineer a contemporary car from the Model-T's debris. Students will see, in the latest car, blocks (structures) borrowed from the wagon.

From this activity, move to a discussion of Derrida's concept of the necessity of using the "already-there," of the need to borrow the engineer's or philosopher's tools (lego/ logo blocks) "if only to destroy" his/her machine (*OG* 139) Legos through legos. Logos through logos.

MASKING TAPE {putting speech in its place}

"The new pedagogy," Ulmer writes, will put speech "in its place in relation to models and mimes, objects and actions" (*AG* 246). In theory, the suppression of speech is easily prescribed; in practice, the challenge is to *do* it. Once, running amuck at the lectern and at wit's end to know how to stop, I grabbed a piece of masking tape and stuck it over my mouth. The effect was to open the classroom to laughter and also, subversive ideas!

Several weeks after the "taping," we read a series of essays interrogating public education, including John Holt's "The Right to Control One's Learning." Persuaded by Holt's radical ideas, the students privately determined to *exercise* their "right to control" their own learning. At a prearranged signal, they produced a rope, tied me to a chair, erased the assignment from the board, and announced a revolution.

All this, in the spirit of play, I submitted to and to *increase* the play, I asked for someone to get me a hamburger with *no mustard*. (Earlier in the course, the students had read an essay on strategies for dealing with terrorists; one suggestion was to make detailed, practical requests). The students' response to my request was to cover my mouth with masking tape. If empowered to play, students know very well how to put speech in its place in relation to action.

MIRROR {self-reflexivity & mirror poems}

No prop works harder in a poststructural classroom than a mirror. When held over a text, mirror-side up, it shows the notion of the book that opens onto and reflects the world; when held mirror-side down over the text, it shows the postmodern notion of writing that reflects only on itself as writing. Gazed into by a male reciting "Bright Star," it shows, as Jan Montefiore demonstrates, the mirror *in the poem*, the woman who reflects and "shows the lover his ideal self" (*Feminism and Poetry* 110).[2] Gazed into by a student told to "Know Thyself," the mirror reveals nothing.

A mirroring material such as tin foil covering a section of the classroom wall reflects the scene of pedagogy and tin foil covering the window of the classroom door suggests pedagogy as a scene that reflects *only* on itself.

PEDESTAL {issues of canonicity & critical desire}

Although hardly standard classroom issue, a large pink plastic pedestal can solve the problem so often posed in our writing: how do we teach the "classics" and simultaneously, interrogate their privileged status, critique their ideologies, and see ourselves in the scene of *academe*? In reality, the challenge is impossible to carry out; we cannot problematize *every* word or idea in a text; some gender issues in *Paradise Lost*, for example, will inevitably go unglossed, even in a reading mediated by Gilbert and Gubar.

What we *can* do, however, is put the book on a pedestal and position the pedestal *dead center* in a classroom circle. This action itself has much to show. Students *see* the putting of the book on the pedestal. They *see* the positioning of the pedestal. They *see* their desks circled like "wagons" around the book to protect and defend it. They see also that the column supporting the book is phallic, that it signifies what Derrida calls "the critical desire" or "the assurance of mastery" (Derrida, *Dissemination*, 230) as the *male* desire.

ROPE {New Critical exegesis}

"The structure of a poem," Cleanth Brooks writes, is like that of a drama or a play. It is not a "formula for action" but an *action*, a series of conflicts, "thrusts," "pressures" which "play against the other" and which must finally be resolved (*The Well-Wrought Urn* 206-210). To perform this scene of conflicting forces (148), divide the class in half, give each side one end of a heavy rope, and engage them in a New Critical tug-of-

---

[2] For her analysis of the mirror-lyric, Montefiore draws on the work of Frederick Goldin in *The Mirror of Narcissus* (Ithaca, N.Y.: Cornell University Press, 1987); elsewhere, she draws attention to Luce Irigaray's *Speculum* and Irigaray's critique of philosophical discourse in which woman "exists to reflect the unified, idealized image of masculine intelligence" (111).

war, e.g., John Ciardi's reading of Frost's "Stopping by Woods on a Snowy Evening":

Side A pulls: Whose woods these are, I think I know
               His house is in the village though
               He will not see me stopping here
               To watch his woods fill up with snow

Side B pulls: My little horse must think it queer
               To stop without a farmhouse near
               Between the woods and frozen lake
               The darkest evening of the year
               He gives his harness bells a shake
               To ask if there is some mistake

Side A pulls: The only other sounds's the sweep
               Of easy wind and down flake
               The woods are lovely dark and deep

Side B pulls: But I have promises to keep
               And miles to go before I sleep.
               And miles to go before I sleep.

In this exercise the students are not free to play freely; their movements are dictated by the New Critical reading of the poem's dramatic structure. The students are expected to suspend their own issues and to tug-and-pull their way to a resolution of the poem's issues. However, anyone who thinks that given a piece of rope, students will *not* play is deluded. In my own classroom, students yanked and pulled their way right out the door and into the hallway.

The rope has other uses, many of which I am still interrogating. If chains are unavailable, a rope can bind together students role-playing as prisoners in Plato's Cave; it can bind books and form knots. It can also serve as a "jump rope" for the re-play of playground litanies.

RUBBER DUCK {repressive linguistic authority}

In her preface to *The Pedagogical Imperative: Teaching as a Literary Genre*, Barbara Johnson teaches a lesson on the "pedagogical dimension" of "The Rime of the Ancient Mariner (iv). According to Johnson, Coleridge's poem offers two views of pedagogy: a view of the lecture as a repressive linguistic authority and a view of the text as the "compulsion to repeat" what we have "not yet understood" (p. vii). Johnson's lesson can

144

be performed by ducking a rubber duck in a basin of water: the ducking represents the scene of the gloss or lecture and the return of the duck, the scene of reading. It is an interesting image to keep in one's head while teaching/ducking, although as one reader observes, the demonstration could also be read as theory's inability to account for the "unsinkable" truth of the text.

SALT SHAKER {the appeal to taste}

A salt shaker shows the appeal to objectivity as the appeal to taste or cultural conditioning. The shaker can show *The Odyssey*, for example, the text for all seasons, as the most seasoned of all texts. (Oregano, basil, or other seasonings, of course, work as well.) To make an *issue* of "taste" one might open a class on the Romantics by sitting on a desk eating honey from a spoon. In the film *Dead Poet's Society*, the teacher, Keating, tells his students that poetry, *good* poetry, has words that "drop from the tongue like honey."

SLATE {the function of imitation}

To deconstruct the function of imitation in the classroom, give a student a child's play slate with eraser and instruct her to record *every word* of a lecture. To comply, the student will be forced periodically to erase. The effect of the exercise is that students see and experience repetition as mindless and futile. The student, of course, may reasonably protest; this demonstration, like many in the propshop, requires trust and the willingness to play.

Slates bound with material and stitched together show the Derridian fold as well as the scene of double writing. Double folding slates, such as the typed used in the 19th century school room, can sometimes be found in antique stores.

SLOTTED SUNGLASSES {grids of intelligibility}

I was inspired to buy a pair of slotted sunglasses while reading Robbe-Grillet's *Jalousie*; looking through the glasses, I imagined I could see "the world" through the eyes of Robbe-Grillet's narrator, as surfaces sliced by *jalousies*. In the classroom, the slots in the glasses function as postmodern grids of intelligibility, i.e., the various theoretical frames, slants, or lenses through which texts currently are read. When seen through the "slots" of feminist theory, for example, Tennyson's "Ulysses" depicts the aging superstar as a man shackled and burdened by an "aging wife."

SNOOPY {summoning play}

There is no text which Snoopy cannot pry open and put into play. Imagine Hamlet and Snoopy prowling around Elsinore, or Snoopy in dark glasses, sitting in his director's chair, directing Hamlet directing *The Murder of Gonzaga*. Derrida of course knows how to open a text but his play is all *work*. Snoopy, as everyone knows, likes to lie on his doghouse and gaze at the stars. Dolls, puppets, and stuffed animals like Snoopy, Belle, or E.T., do *not*, as some might argue, infantilize; they summon play, and play, as any child knows, imperils and involves risk. In my classroom is a box filled with stuffed animals; students, females *and* males, "nerds" *and* "jocks," vie for their favorites and "prop" them beside them in their seats. Speaking to and through the stuffed animals, students can vent their feelings as well as pitch their voices "differently."

STEREOSCOPE {history without footnotes}

The effect of viewing a nineteenth century parlor through the lens of a stereoscope can be, as Adrienne Rich suggests, quite terrifying:

> Last night we sat with the stereopticon,[3]
> laughing at genre views of 1906,
> till suddenly, gazing straight into
> that fringed and tasselled parlor, where the vestal
> spurns an unlikely suitor
> with hairy-crested plants to right and left,
> my heart sank. It was terrible.
> I smelled the mildew in those swags of plush,
> ("Readings of History," *Snapshots* 36)

The theme of most stereoscopic scenes is domestic humor; in the frozen fetishes and exotic details of the Victorian parlor, however, there is much to mystify: screens, busts, draperies, dancing dogs, spiked plants, wallpapers, stuffed heads, imported birds, feathers. The scene is history, but "without footnotes" (Thomas 187).

TELEVISION REMOTE CONTROLS {formatting the text for t.v.}

As a prop for a scene performed in class, one of my students made, from construction paper, a television remote control. I appropriated it and immediately put it to use, zapping the students like a t.v.. The grammar

---

[3] The details in Rich's poem suggest the *stereoscope*, not the *stereogticon*. A *stereogticon*, according to Webster's, is a magic lantern which produces dissolving views.

and syntax of this scene, the students knew better than I: "Zap me! ""Zap me!" they cried, vying to enact fragments of weather reports, soaps, crime dramas, news shows, game shows, commercials, and exercise routines. The responses were playful, noisy, and instructive.

Later, in a lacklustre class discussion of *Oedipus Rex*, I produced the remote control and again zapped the class, invited the students to "turn on the t.v., "to pivot or turn from a classroom discussion of the text to a discussion of the text as formatted by television.

After much pointing and pumping, a student finally responded. Simulating a t.v. newsbreak, he said: "We interrupt this program to bring you a special announcement. CNN has just learned that Oedipus married his mother."

"Oprah Winfrey!" a student interrupted, inspired. "This family should be on Oprah. It's totally dysfunctional. Can I be Oprah?"

"Can I be Oedipus?"

"Can I be the person who wrote a book?"

Bringing the literary text into the format of a television talk show not only gives students a ready-made forum for discussion; it also gives them access to voices and issues "outside" the classroom.

TOOTHPICKS {meaning as a function of difference}

The idea that meaning is a function not of the signified but of the difference between signifiers, is difficult for students for grasp. A simple exercise performed with toothpicks helped my students *see* the Saussurian "difference." I gave the students several toothpicks each and asked them to use the toothpicks to write their names, breaking the toothpicks if necessary.

"Imagine I am an alien," I said, squinting and frowning at the toothpick arrangements on the desks. "I can't read your alphabet, but I do know I am looking at the scene of *writing*. Why?"

The students studied at their toothpick arrangements. "Repetition," one said. "They repeat."

"What else?" I asked.

"The way they're spaced."

"The way they relate to each other."

"They're at angles."

"Put one toothpick directly on top of another one. What happens to the 'writing'," I asked.

"It disappears."

"So meaning is not in the toothpick: meaning is a function of the *difference*, the spaces between the toothpicks."

"Yes, but so what? You still don't know what the writing *means*."

"That's not the point."

URN {destructing the proposition}

An inexpensive pottery urn—of the type sold in dimestores, preferably one embellished by a rural scene—can interrogate the "truth" of Keats' famous proposition, "A thing of beauty is a joy forever." As a preface to this demonstration, read the opening lines of *Endymion*, display the urn, then hurl it against the wall. Contrary to Keats' proposition, the urn's "beauty," i.e., the concept of beauty represented by the urn, will "pass into nothingness.'' That the breaking of icons is not without *violence* and *cost* are points to consider as is the notion of a beauty that is ahistorical and transcendent of culture, race, gender, and class. *Against* this experiment are arguments which students may themselves uncover.

YARDSTICK {taking measure of the metaphysical}

In a text favored by teachers of Advanced Placement English, Laurence Perrine writes: "The measurement of a poem is a much more complex process, of course, than is the measurement of a rectangle. It cannot be done as exactly" (731). To show students the appeal to metaphysics, take the measurement, in *The Norton Anthology of Literature by Women*, of Elizabeth Barrett Browning's "How do I love thee?" (276). The height of the sonnet is precisely two inches; the length of its longest line is two and five/eighths inches. This demonstration shows students that what Perrine terms a "complex process" is not a process in measurement; the appeal is elsewhere, to aesthetic *taste*. The yardstick cannot measure what it cannot see; unlike the speaker in Elizabeth Barrett Browning's famous sonnet, it cannot take the "depth and breadth and height" of things "out of sight."

Nor can the yardstick mark the end of a propshop. Some of my favorite pedagogical objects—a black box, gauze, a bag of marbles, a measuring cup, play money, a "bee" hand puppet and flyswatter (to put the "be" under erasure), paper fan—I have, in the interest of space, omitted. Others suggest themselves even as I write. I am thinking now, for example, of how women historically have bracketed off or framed a piece of embroidery or sewing with *hoops*. I am certain that in a toystore, I can find a child's set of sized embroidery hoops along with a bit of fabric. The fabric will show the text of Poe's story, "The Purloined Letter"; the smaller hoop, Lacan's framing; and the larger hoop, Derrida's. Framing, of course, is a *woman's* art, as is embroidery (narration), and sewing (sowing). To show the scene of dissemination and sowing, I have, in the past, blown dandelion seeds into the classroom, but alas, no dandelion has ever sprouted there. In the future, I will sow more *productively*, with needle and thread.

Our props, of course, read us. Mine, a friend tells me, betray a desire to domesticate theory, to use objects that comfort students and give them a place; to take them out of the "angst and agon of *Critical Inquiry* and allow them to feel at home." And as my friend went on to point out, it is when students feel at home that they feel they can play and be 'subversive' and really make the texts theirs.

Mary Alice Delia

Epilogue

(from the original 1991 dissertation)

KILLER ENGLISH: POSTMODERN THEORY

AND THE HIGH SCHOOL CLASSROOM

by

Mary Alice Delia

Dissertation submitted to the Faculty of the Graduate School
of The University of Maryland in partial fulfillment
of the requirements for the degree of
Doctor of Philosophy
1991

Advisory Committee:

Professor Susan A. Handelman, Chairperson/Advisor
Associate Professor Susan S. Lanser
Assistant Professor John Schilb
Professor Theresa Coletti
Associate Professor James Greenberg

Epilogue

I now depart the university to return to the high
school classroom. Under the terms of my academic leave, I
am sure of a position, but the assignment itself is not
guaranteed and while writing the last pages of this
dissertation, I have also been going through the process of
the interview. In each of three interviews thus far, I have
been asked the same two questions:

1. If we were to observe your classroom, what would we most
    likely see?
2. What are your strategies for motivating students?

While much could be written of and in response to these
questions, I would like, leaving _academe_, to make two
observations. The first is that the questions focus almost
exclusively on classroom practice. The second is that
because candidates are ranked on the basis of their
responses, the questions suggest that some classroom
practices are more desirable, more valuable than others.

I believe the questions are the right questions and
that all in all, they are fair. Concerns about classroom
practice _should_ lie at the heart of an interview conducted
in an institution of learning, regardless of level. It may

be appropriate, at the college or university level, to inquire also about publications, awards, grants, degrees, projections for books. But there is no question more important than the one that asks what we do in the classroom, how we motivate students, how we teach.

And certainly some teaching practices are more effective than others. Just as some readings include more information, more arguments, counter-arguments, more consideration of "difference," so some teaching practices evidence more strategies for motivating students and for analyzing resistance; more knowledge of learning theory, more understanding of learning styles, more techniques, in other words, for fostering cognitive growth.

In a truly dynamic pedagogical practice, however, there is something radically in excess of what can be measured and assessed. Analyzing my own experience as a student writing this dissertation, I think this "something" derives from the teacher's willingness or determination to value the ideas of students as much as her own, to find, in the thoughts and ideas of the other, that which is treasurable, delightful, worth pursuing. In writing this dissertation, I have focused on the ability of postmodern theory to empower students, but here, in the epilogue, I understand how critical it is for students to know they can empower their teachers. What a difference it makes when one sees with her

own eyes that her words have made a difference to the
teacher, have excited _her_ imagination, have empowered _her_!
Such moments are difficult to describe in the abstract, bu
they can be seen, perhaps, and perhaps _only_ in the letter.

August 1, 1991

Dear Professor Schilb:

Never having met you, I had no idea, that day in the
South Dining Hall, what to expect. For all I knew, you
might have been an absolute tyrant. But not two minutes
into my pizza, I was sketching a church and a courthouse on
a paper napkin.

"So I said to the kids, are you saying Marion Barry
should _confess_ his _crime_? 'Where should he go to _do_ this'
I asked them, 'to the church or the court house'? Well! Dic
that get them going!"

Then I thought to myself, "Oh, Oh. Now you've done it.
He'll think you're a screwball."

But you burst out laughing. "Terrific!" you said. "Could
you put those in your dissertation--just like that, the way
you've drawn them?"

Do you know how _empowering_ that was? Thank you.

August 3, 1991

Dear Professor Lanser:

One mid-winter afternoon we were in your office,
talking about the three completed chapters. "As critiques
of the academy, these chapters are fine," you said, "but
what _I_ would like to know is, how would you do it
differently? When are you going to write about how _you_
teach, what _you_ do in the classroom?"

I was taken aback, even embarrassed. "Who would be
interested in what _I_ do?"

"Me!" you said emphatically.

"Really?"

"Yes! I would love to know what you do. I really
would." I could see with my own eyes that you were sincere.
Thirty years of feeling "secondary" slid down the drain.
You really did want to know. Well! I shot home on the
Beltway and began Chapter Four.

For that, I truly thank you.

                                        August 4, 1991

Dear Professor Handelman:

     One has only to pack a few boxes with a teacher packing
a few boxes for another teacher unable, because of illness,
to pack his own, to know how precious she regards the books,
papers, desk items, lamps, wall hangings of the "other,"
right down to the paper clips!

     And I have only to read again, your letters about the
The Dead Poets Society paper to see "with my own eyes" that
if you urged me to throw the paper away and "teach," it is
because you really did believe I had something "unique" to
add.

     When I floundered, when on at least one occasion, I was
in over my head, you added your voice to my own and pulled
me through.

     Most important, you did not judge or try to recruit me;
you had confidence in my own project and you helped me. You
are the one who has helped me to understand my practice, who
has given me the tools to shape and theorize it in the same
way as, from the beginning, you have believed in and helped
me to write this dissertation. How is it possible to
acknowledge so much?

     Because in my opinion, even Derrida would have
difficulty finding the right words to thank you, I now
understand that there is, that there must be, as you say,
"a word beyond the word."

                                   As ever,

                                   Mary Alice

Afterword

Susan Handelman, Professor Emerita, Department of English,

Bar-Ilan University, Israel

The Epilogue to this book, *Killer English*, concludes with the Epilogue that Mary Alice wrote to her own PhD dissertation in 1991. At the end of it, she copied individual letters of gratitude she wrote to the three members of her dissertation committee, of which I was the Director. So what better way for me to add an Afterword to this book, than also with a letter to her. I copied below selections from one I wrote in December 1997 as my way of contributing to the Memorial service organized by her friends, colleagues, and former students, after she had passed away a month before. (I was abroad on a sabbatical in Israel at the time.)

First, though, a few words of preface to that letter.

When I met her, Mary Alice was an older adult coming to the University of Maryland College Park for a PhD after a decades long award -winning career as a High School English teacher. She had been trained in the culture of literary studies, and education of the 50s and 60s. The "New Criticism" of that time was formalistic, apolitical, hierarchical. As I look back, I think what the new Literary Theory of the 1980s and 1990s she studied with us at Maryland did for her was to fully liberate her extraordinary pedagogical genius. And even more, it also freed her as a woman who had grown up in the previous generation, with so many constraints on choice of career, and narrow definitions of what was acceptable for females. In all the years she was my graduate student—in fact, in every week of every graduate seminar she took with me, and in every letter she wrote to me as we discussed ongoing chapters of her dissertation — I could feel viscerally how all she was learning, was like air and oxygen to somebody gasping for it.

If she were to be writing a dissertation today, I imagine her swallowing every new idea in the field of literary study, and from them creating pedagogical scenarios that would still make us laugh, applaud, and be astounded at her insight and ability to activate her students, to make it all come alive, and fulfill her desire to change the world.

She and I continued to correspond as friends and colleagues from after she received her PhD in 1991 until her passing in 1997. How moving it was to receive, one day 25 years later, an email from her son Joe, about his rediscovery of her PhD dissertation, and new interest in her ideas. And to hear his warm memories of how she spoke of her relationship with me. I encouraged Joe to continue what I had also been working on with her before her passing: getting her dissertation revised and published. In these past few years of his working on this project with extraordinary dedication and love, I felt graced by her reappearance in my life, and the new connection with her family, of whom she used to speak of so much to me.

As my Afterword, I copy below selections from the "Letter to Mary Alice" written on December 20, 1997 for the Memorial event a month after her passing. That letter was written for a sad occasion, but about all the gifts of life she had given to me, her colleagues, friends, and students. How pleased I am that now, decades later, it has become a letter for a joyful occasion, in honor of a new birth of her life, one that will spread her gifts to many others: this book *Killer English*.

****

Dear Mary Alice:

You always wrote me such wonderful letters. Letters were so much the basis of our friendship, and then became part of the creative pedagogy we worked out together. So I know you would so enjoy my writing this memorial for you in the form of a letter. But even more than that: I feel that for me, our correspondence, our relationship, will never end.

Can it be already 14 years since we first met— when you came back to graduate school at the University of Maryland in 1985 and took seminars on literary theory with me? I was your professor, but soon I became *your* student, for I learned so much from you about teaching. You taught me by fully embodying how a good teacher is always the student of her students. Trying to understand them, worrying about them, learning from them. You were my student and my teacher. And you always will be.

The day before I learned of your passing, I was sitting with one of my colleagues here in Jerusalem on my sabbatical and talking about you. We were working on methods for teaching classical Jewish and Rabbinic texts to adults without background. I started telling him all about you. About how when I had to teach courses on the Bible, I always turned to you for suggestions of how to really grab my students: What to do with the Adam and Eve story? Back came a list from you with 10 ideas, such as "Bring in a bag of old barbecued rib bones and some putty and fabric ask the men in the class to 'construct the rib into a female'; have the women watch and ask them what they think and feel." Garden of Eden and the Snake? "Bring in some special chocolate or treat, and put some at each student's place and tell them "you are forbidden to eat this." Then go on with the class as usual. In the middle, ask them what they were thinking and feeling."

I could go on and on. Your classroom was so full of wit, joy, playfulness. When we would talk together about your teaching ideas, you would always flash that wonderful wide-eyed smile of yours, and let out that distinctive throaty laugh. You were as fresh and eager after 37 years of teaching as the newest Education School graduate.

I always gave out chapters of your PhD dissertation on literary theory and the teaching of English to the graduate students in my other seminars. To show them they did not have to abandon their love and concern for pedagogy in order to become serious academics. Several of them wrote me last week: "We all felt so sad when we heard about Mary Alice. We talked a lot about her work, and how important it was for all of us. It gave us, we felt, a sense that rigorous scholarship and the stuff we love CAN work together. It was very important to know."

We continued to write to each other long after you finished your PhD with me. The last e-mail I wrote you was this past September. It was a long description of my life on my fellowship here in Israel… You wrote me back, in the very last e-mail I received for you this past October, and also described your experiences trying to teach again while coping with your illness:

"I developed migraines and had to cut my fall teaching to one course, a survey of British Lit. since the 1800's. To tell you the truth, I'm having a hard time making it through to the end of even this one course—the day after I teach, I usually spend in bed! I didn't think I was doing such a hot job this semester but one of my students is on the UNCW paper and she nominated me for "Professor of the Week" and lo and behold, that's all it took! I couldn't believe it, being lowly part-time and having taught there only a year and a half. The English Department made a big deal out of it—put the article "under glass" and so forth. That accolade is only part of the story of this course, however; some of the students are NOT having a good time in the class and for good reason—I'm doing too much lecturing and traditional stuff and I know it. It's just that I feel the pressure of covering so much ground in one semester ... The problem is endemic to the survey course, I guess.... [I try] to ... make the material intensely relevant, up close and personal - with Shelley's idea of the poet-legislator, e.g., I ask whom they would rather have as President: Bill Gates or Robert Frost?

I'm not teaching next semester and am thinking seriously of not doing it any more at all. It's just too scary, wondering if I'll be able to finish the course or attend all the classes, or get sick IN class. And I think, Why? Why put myself through all that? The answer unfortunately is too obvious - because teaching keeps me connected, encourages me to grow mentally, gives me problems to solve, makes possible new relationships...."

That was you, Mary Alice, the consummate teacher, always worrying about and rethinking her classes, always beloved by her students, always passing on a word of support and encouragement to your friends. And how ironic, that the letter I am writing now is for *your* memorial service.

It is also ironic that the day I was talking about you to my colleague here in Jerusalem, the last day of your life in this world, he and I were also examining texts from the Bible and Jewish tradition about various forms of leave-taking, and about teachers and students. We were looking at the ways the greatest teacher in the Bible, Moses, responds to God's telling him at the end of the book of Deuteronomy that the time has come for him to leave the world, and that he would not be able to go into the Promised Land...

Mary Alice, you too, were our teacher. Like Moses in this story, it must have been so painful for you to have stop teaching, to leave your students, to have to withdraw, not to go all the way to the Promised Land...

I wrote to your husband Frank after hearing news of your passing: "I feel very privileged to have known Mary Alice. I will never forget her. Here in Jerusalem, the focus of so much spiritual yearning, so much agonizing history, so many hopes for a future redemption, one somehow feels the presence of those who have passed on...heaven is a little closer to earth here. After Mary Alice became ill, I always included her in my prayers. I will continue to remember her soul. You took wonderful care of her. May her memory always be a source of joy and blessing for all of us."

Love,
Susan Handelman

Appendix A

News Clippings for Analysis

1. In the past, team members asserted that they readily gave access to the unpublished texts to other scholars. But they use a form of doublespeak. What they mean by access is that if you know which document to ask for (there is no published catalogue of the secret documents, and even if you knew the name of a document you would not necessarily know whether it was relevant to your work) and if you ask the individual team editor assigned to publish it (the man with the biggest hoard-J.T. Milik in Paris-doesn't answer mail) and if he decides that you are a competent, deserving scholar, and if you go to where he has his photograph, you see it *provided* you don't publish the text.

    — Hershel Shanks, "The Dead Sea Scroll Monopoly" *Washington Post* October 8, 1991: A19.

2. Ladies and gentlemen, I am about to provide you with a pair of demonstrations that should, I would fervently hope, forever turn you away from such a disgusting and unnatural food as this. I say "disgusting" because of its high bacterial content—a content I will show to be equal to or greater than that of barnyard ordure—and I say "unnatural" because this flesh food is an innovation and corruption of modern man, whose ancestors have been proven to be exclusively frugivorous. And, too, I will assert that such foods are in fact "sinful," not only in the sin occasioned by the taking of the lives of our fellow creatures but in the very greatest sin of all, that is, of course, in polluting the temple of the human body.

    — T. Coraghessan Boyle, "Monday Night at the Temple of Health." *New York Times*, April 7, 1993 Op-Ed: A15.

3. When pregnant women seek prenatal treatment at the hospital, staff members choose those whom they suspect of being drug users and, without informing the women, test them for drug use. If the test is positive, the woman is threatened with jail unless she signs up for treatment, agrees to have continuing drug tests and agrees to complete both drug treatment and prenatal care that the hospital prescribes.

— Philip J. Hilts, "Hospital Is Object of Rights Inquiry." *New York Times* February 6, 1994: 29.

4. Suspended students at Martin Luther King Jr. Middle School in Germantown have learned to bring cups of drinking water to the suspension room because they are allowed only two breaks during the 6 1/2-hour day, and then only to go to the restroom. The rest of the time, they must complete schoolwork in silence … With a parent' s permission, Steinberg [principal] said, he sentences some students to 'school service 'with the janitorial crew because 'our philosophy is that when you get into a fight, you damage the school climate. So, to clean your record, you literally have to clean the school.'

— Dan Beyers, "Suspended Students Not Always Sent Home." *Washington Post* April 16, 1995: Al.

5. It is a humbling realization that the number of ways that children can conceal their actions from their parents cannot be enumerated in any reasonable lifetime .... Parenthood is a continual struggle to define the line that divides proper attention to trust and privacy from excessive gullibility that parents fear could lead to a shattered life. It is the pain, the ambiguity and the uncertainty of this decision making that may cause parents at their wit's end to choose Drug Alert.

— Frank Kizer, "Mom and Dad's Choice." *Washington Post* April 21, 1995. Letter to the Editor.[1]

---

[1] Written in response to the attack in "Mom and Dad: Agents of Big Brother?" (April 9), on DrugAlert, a product enabling parents to check children 's bedrooms (clothing, possessions) for evidence of drug-use.

Appendix B

Questions & Answers for Role-Play as Patients and Staff in a Mental Health Facility

The material is taken from "Mental Health Rights ...and Wrongs, "a handbook produced in 1988 by the Maryland Disability Law Center, Inc., a state agency for the mentally ill created in response to Public Law 99-319, the Protection and Advocacy for Mentally Ill Individuals Act.

Forced Medication

Q. Can I refuse to take medication?

A. If you are involuntarily committed or committed by a court for treatment, you may be given medication against your will if the medication is approved by a 'Clinical Review Panel', subject to your right to appeal.

You have the right to be represented by a 'lay advi'sor.' This is a hospital employee who is knowledgeable about mental health practice and whose job it is to help patients with rights complaints.

Q. Can I be represented by a lawyer or another person at the Clinical Review Panel instead of the lay advisor?

A. The law is silent on this point. You can ask the hospital to allow you to have a lawyer or other person of your choice represent you. But the hospital can say no.

Access to Medical Records

Q. Can I see my medical records?

A. Your right to see portions of your records may be limited by a physician only if the physician determines that it would be harmful to your treatment to see *specific* information in your files.

Privacy of Records

Q. Are my records private?

A. Yes. Your records at the facility are confidential. They cannot be given to anyone except people you authorize to see them. There are a few minor exceptions to this rule. Your records can be reviewed by government officials who license the hospital, for example, but those government officials must keep the information private.

Conditional Release

Q. What is a conditional release?

A. Conditional release means that you will be allowed to live outside of the facility only if you comply with the conditions about care and treatment that are set by the facility. These conditions may be that you attend a certain day program or live in a certain place. The facility can state how long the conditional release will last. The law about the effect of a conditional release and the kinds of conditions the facility can set upon your freedom once you are released is not clear.

Visitors

Q. Can friends and relatives visit me?

A. Yes. There is (only) one limitation on your right to have visitors. If it is medically justifiable, a physician may restrict visits or private conversations.

Letters

Q. Can I receive and send letters?

A. Each facility must provide you with access to pens or pencils, paper, envelopes and stamps so that you can write letters. Your letters must be mailed without delay by the facility.   Also, the staff may not open and read the mail you send. However, Maryland law currently provides that the facility may open your outgoing mail if the person to whom your letter is addressed requests it.

Facility Routine and Rules

Q. When can my freedom in the facility be taken away?

A. Most treatment facilities use a system in which residents must earn certain 'privileges 'by acting in a certain manner. 'Privileges' often include trips outside of the facility, freedom to leave the unit unescorted, and 'grounds privileges'—being outside. Residents frequently complain that the privilege system is unfair or that their privileges have been unfairly denied.

The law is not settled on the limits that can be placed on daily activities of individuals who are voluntarily or involuntarily admitted to impatient facilities ... Many advocates for the rights of persons who are labelled mentally ill and treatment providers disagree on the need for and the appropriate limits of restrictions on residents 'rights and freedoms within facilities.

Grievance Procedures

Q. What is the grievance procedure used in state hospitals?

A. If you are in a state facility and you think one of your rights has been violated, you can file a complaint through the Resident Grievance System.

Step 1:   Complain to the Rights Advisor

Step 2:   Appeal to the Unit Director

Step 3:   Appeal to the Superintendent or the Clients 'Rights Committee

Step 4:   Appeal to the Central Review Committee

Q. Who can help me with this complaint process?

A. The Rights Advisor is required to help you through the process and tell you at each step what your rights are and what the next step is.

Mary Alice Delia

Appendix C

Excerpts from American Literary Histories

From the Preface to *Cyclopaedia of American Literature* by Evert A. Duyckinck and George L. Duyckinck. In Two Volumes. New York: Charles Scribner, 1855.

The design of the Cyclopaedia is to bring together as far as possible in one book convenient for perusal and reference, memorials and records of the writers of the country and their works, from the earliest period to the present day. In the public and private library, it is desirable to have at hand the means of information on a number of topics which associate themselves with the lives of persons connected with literature. There are numerous points of this kind, not merely relating to authorship, but extending into the sphere of social and political life, which are to be sought for in literary biography, and particularly in the literary biography of America, where the use of the pen has been for the most part incidental to other pursuits. The history of the literature of the country involved in the pages of this work, is not so much an exhibition of art and invention, of literature in its immediate and philosophical sense, as a record of mental progress and cultivation, of facts and opinions, which derives its main interest from its historical rather than its critical value. It is important to know what books have been produced, and by whom; whatever the books may have been or whoever the men.

From the Preface to *A Manual of American Literature: A Text-Book for Schools and Colleges,* by John S. Hart, LL.D. Philadelphia: Eldredge Brother, 1872.

The systematic study of English literature, as part of the course of ordinary English education, has been introduced almost entirely with the last thirty years... Hardly a school of any standing is now to be found that does not include the systematic study of English Literature in its ordinary curriculum. The study has come to be considered almost as necessary as that of Grammar and Geography, and fully as necessary as that of History. The study of Literature is in fact a part of the study of History ... The latest step in this onward movement is that which recognizes the propriety of giving a full and adequate treatment to the literature of our own country. The volume now in the hands of the reader furnishes ample proof, if any were needed, that American Literature is abundant in materials, and that it is growing with unexampled rapidity.

From "The Distinctive Purpose and Plan of This Volume" *The Literature of America and Our Favorite Authors*, ed. William Wilfred Birdsall and Rufus M. Jones. Seattle, Washington: Chapman Bros. & Co., 1897.

The first and main purpose of the work is to present to our American homes a mass of wholesome, varied and well-selected reading matter. In this respect it is substantially a volume for the family. America is pre-eminently a country of homes. These homes are the schools of citizenship, and—next to the Bible, which is the foundation of our morals and laws—we need those books which at once entertain and instruct, and, at the same time, stimulate patriotism and pride for our native land.

From the Introduction to *An American Anthology*: 1787-1900, ed. Edmund Clarence Stedman. New York: Houghton, Mifflin and Company, 1900.

Our own poetry excels as a recognizable voice in utterance of a people. The storm and stress of youth have been upon us, and the nation has not lacked its lyric cry; meanwhile the typical sentiments of piety, domesticity, freedom, have made our less impassioned verse at least sincere. One who underrates the significance of our literature, prose or verse, as both the expression and the stimulant of national feeling, as of import in the past and to the future of America, and therefore of the world, is deficient in that critical insights which can judge even of its own day unwarped by personal taste or deference to public impression. He shuts his eyes to the fact that at times, notably throughout the years resulting in the Civil War, this literature has been a 'force.'

From the Introduction to *A Literary History of America* by Barrett Wendell. New York: Charles Scribner's Sons, 1900.

Yet, English or not, we Americans are English-speaking still; and English-speaking we must always remain. An accident of language and nothing more, this fact may seem to many. To those who think more deeply it can hardly fail to mean that for better or worse the ideals which underlie our blundering conscious life must always be the ideals which underlie the conscious life of the mother country, and which for centuries have rectified and purified her blunders. Morally and religiously these ideals are immortally consecrated in King James's version of the Bible; legally and politically these ideals are grouped in that great legal system which, in distinction from the Canon Law of the Civil, may broadly be called the Common Law of English. What these ideals are, everyone bred in the traditions of our ancestral language instinctively knows; but such knowledge is hard to phrase. Perhaps we come as near as may be to truth when we say that in their moral aspect the ideals which underlie our language are comprised in a profound conviction that, whatever our station or our shortcomings, each of us is bound to do right; and that in their legal aspect these ideals may similarly be summarised in the statement that we are bound on earth to maintain our rights.

From the Preface to *American Literature* by John Calvin Metcalf (Johnson Publishing Company: Richmond, Virginia, 1914).

In this work an attempt is made to present in a clear and systematic manner the main facts and tendencies in American literature from the beginnings to the present. Special emphasis has been given to movements and individual characteristics which seem distinctively American. We are beginning to realize at last the American literature is not merely an off-shoot from English literature, but that it is in a larger and truer sense a record of national traits and strivings for at least a century and a quarter. Even the Colonial and Revolutionary periods, in which no great literature was produced, are exceedingly important as a background for the proper estimate of our later literature and should not be neglected by the serious student of American institutions.

After the first two periods it would be a difficult task indeed to classify our authors on a uniform national basis. They are all American, of course, but they flourished mainly in groups and by sections; when one attempts to consider them, it is the most natural thing in the world to arrange them geographically according to their development; any other arrangement, it seems to the present writer, would be confusing. What the student has a right to demand in a textbook above everything else is clearness of presentation; and the history of literature in a big country like ours, where diversity of interest and tradition only serves to give a spice of variety to our essential national unity, cannot be clearly and truthfully presented except along the lines of its natural growth. This is not sectionalism, but diversified Americanism. The contribution of New English, with its strong moral and didactic flavor; of the Middle States,

171

with their more metropolitan tendencies; of the South, with its romantic sentiment; of the West, with its fresh and vigorous reality; — each of these contributions is set forth as a significant element in our national development. Perhaps the most striking thing in our literary history is the picturesqueness of these several contributions, merging into a larger union of common interests. To lose sight of this characteristic of American literature is to fail to apprehend its deeper meaning.

From the Foreword to *The American Spirit in Letters*, by Stanley Thomas Williams. New Haven: Yale University Press, 1926.

In the sense in which the anthropologist uses the term, the United States and Europe have become part of the same culture area. America, three hundred years ago on the periphery of this area, has, in the twentieth century, become a part of its dynamic center. The period of isolation and of tutelage has passed. As never before in our national history, the forces that are molding the development of Europe are molding also the life of the transatlantic republic. Industrialism, Socialism and Christianity are but a few of the forces common to the peoples of the western world. Americans are becoming conscious of their new world situation and of the international character of many of the factors with which they have to reckon. They are making adjustments to these new conditions. As yet American literature of the twentieth century seems to be largely national and, since the World War, iconoclastic. It has been in harmony with a trend toward an intense national consciousness that has been an outstanding characteristic of twentieth-century American. Perhaps it is too soon for men of letters to grapple with the implications of the fact that America is one of the small group of very powerful nations. American writers, in the main, seem content to display the pettiness, the credulities, and the absurdities of Americans. They have declared their intention that American literature shall stand on its own feet. So speaks the nationalist in almost every country of the world. The American movement has its counterpart in many other lands. He would be a bold man who would undertake to prophesy what will come of all this nationalism and industrialism. There are some who see a little way ahead limitless opportunities for development, and, for America, increasing power. Others cannot escape the haunting specter of a world debacle. With anticipation mingled with apprehension we push forward into the unknown.

Appendix D

Precinct 101 Investigative Procedures Manual

STRATEGIES AND PROCEDURES FOR

INTERROGATING TEXTS

Section D.1: Text Profiles. Composites. & SOP

The suspect in this case is the literary text. It is believed that the literary text has certain social or cultural connections that it is trying to cover up or conceal. The literary text denies these connections; it claims it is an art object and not a sociological or cultural document. As a new historicist interrogator, your job is to find evidence of the text's cultural transactions. Begin by reading the text closely, looking for tell-tale links and overlappings between concepts and ideas in its language and the discourse of other cultural documents and archives in the time period, e.g., newspapers, ledgers, chronicles, minutes, broadsides, notices, gazettes, journals, logs, periodicals, laws, notices, billboards, cook books, compendiums.[1]

Be alert to the fact that "highbrow" literary texts are skilled disguisers of cultural connections. Texts of the very highest literary importance are especially tough cases and will be difficult, if not impossible, to crack. These texts are adept at using formal elements as smokescreens to conceal their cultural anxieties. *The Scarlet Letter*, for example, claims to be "about" events in the seventeenth century but it was written in 1849, just prior to the outbreak of the Civil War. That Hawthorne had opinions about issues important to this war is known from his journals and letters; nowhere in *The Scarlet Letter* are these opinions explicitly voiced but in a

---

[1] For an excellent discussion of Foucault's research methodology, see Deleuze's "A New Archivist" (*Foucault* 1-22), especially pages 15-17.

novel saturated with anxieties and issues of freedom, rebellion, servitude, and bondage, Hawthorne's own "Civil War" opinions are surely present.

Not all texts are masters of disguise; some (perhaps short story installments), if followed carefully, might eventually show their social and/or political connections quite openly. Poe's story "The Mystery of Marie Roget," for example, is a case in point. A former student-investigator discovered that when the story was first published in the November, 1842 *Ladies' Home Companion*, it was prefaced by a quotation from Von Hardenburg, which was printed both in German and in English. Interestingly, the German version is absent in the 1943 edition but reappears in publications copyrighted after 1965.[2] As the student also noted, the German version of the Von Hardenburg quotation is not the only passage in Poe's story that disappears for reasons that seemingly have nothing to do with "literature." According to this student's research, "the last segment of Poe's story was withheld for a month because the police had gained new information regarding the case of Mary Rogers. Poe had to wait and see if the real murder would be solved."[3] (A detailed description of this student's report follows later.)

Section D.2: Surveillance Techniques

Follow the literary text to gain familiarity with its characters, plot, setting, language, and so forth, but more important to the new historicist investigation, note carefully those aspects of the text that you do *not* understand. Read to construct but also to frustrate meaning, to follow the obvious leads, cues, and directives, but at the same time, to note (and zoom in on) details, words, facts, allusions, or topical references whose meaning and significance elude you. Precisely there, in the unfamiliar, may be the link to contemporary cultural or social anxieties. Early in *A Farewell to Arms*, for example, Henry asks a wounded soldier, "Were you in the States?" "Sure," the soldier replies, "In Pittsburgh." Why

---

[2] From a March 26, 1992, report submitted by an eleventh-grade student, Alia Williams.
[3] The story of the relation of Poe's story to the story of the murder of one Mary Cecilia Rogers is fascinating and one an entire class might profitably investigate. Included in its intertext is a heady new historicist mix of documents and archival material: newspaper accounts of the murder, police statements and reports, Poe's editor's statements, Poe's statements, and later, Raymond Paul's 1971 *Who Murdered Mary Rogers?* and of course countless articles and references elsewhere. In addition to providing students with a *real* mystery to speculate on (and perhaps solve?), the case shows clearly the connectedness and interdependency of literature, culture, society, and history.

Pittsburgh? What, in the 1920's, was perceived as essentially "American" about Pittsburgh? Why not New York or Philadelphia?

For more clues to the text's cultural, social, and political connections, read its early reviews. Consider, for example, this excerpt from an 1896 review praising Dickinson and Whitman for their "markedly American" outlook:

> Her outlook upon Death (and Walt Whitman's also) is so calm, so nonchalant; her pride so near Yankee brag; her seriousness so close to Yankee humor; so fond of every-day things, in short, so bigly democratic, that I feel in the poetry of both of them something markedly American, something majestic that belongs especially over here in our United States. (Chelifer 543)

Or, this 1858 *Atlantic Monthly* passage praising Emerson for his Yankee inventiveness and comparing the philosophical inquiry to the American quest for patentable ideas:

> The inventiveness which characterizes Americans, the multiplicity of patents, comes for the tendency to go behind the actual, to test possibilities, to bring everything to the standard of thought. Emerson dissolves English in the alembic of his brain, and makes a thought of that. ("The New World…526).

Read also (text-tap) the writer's autobiographical accounts, personal papers, letters, missives, diaries, publishing contracts, and all other correspondence and records of correspondence you can uncover and track down. Attitudes, biases, and assumptions operating as formalist elements in the so-called literary text often show themselves openly in documents of a more "private" nature. In a 1923 letter from Fitzgerald to Tom Boyd, for example, a former student-investigator found the following statement: "All the marvelous places like Majoca turn out to have one enormous disadvantage—bugs, lepers, Jews, consumptives, or philistines." Returning to his reading of *The Great Gatsby*, the student concludes:

> Fitzgerald's dislike of Jews is shown in his portrayal of Wolfsheim. Wolfsheim has stereotypical Jewish looks and also acts like a stereotypical Jew. Most important in this stereotype is the fact that Wolfsheim is a conspirator, and in the worst sense of the word. Wolfsheim conspired to fix the 1919 World Series. He played "with the faith of fifty million people—with the single mindedness of a burglar robbing a safe (Fitzgerald 74). A key factor here is who these fifty-

million people are. They are the American people, and Fitzgerald is pointing out that Jews like Wolfsheim have no respect for American ideals or values like baseball ... they are inherently unAmerican and shouldn't be here in the first place.[4]

Section D.3: Verification Procedures

Regardless of the text's canonical status, check out and verify its story. Do not accept its account of things at face value. Read materials published in the same period that tell its "Facts" differently or from another perspective. Steinbeck's *Cannery Row*, for example, set in the Great Depression, presents self-sufficient, colorful characters (down-and-out-doctor, heart-as-good-as-gold prostitute). Other accounts of the canneries during that time period, e.g., union reports or newspaper articles, might challenge the "romance" of Steinbeck's story. Read to learn how plot, theme, character, setting —elements we call *literary* — behave, perform, play out elsewhere, e.g., the plot of a *real* whaling voyage, or the characters in a *real* Missouri river town in 1840.

Along with individual texts, words and titles associated with literary periods and/or groups of writers should be rigorously interrogated. Hemingway and Fitzgerald, for example, along with other "disillusioned" novelists of the 1920's are referred to in literary circles as the "lost generation" and are revered for their critiques of America in the years following World War I. As a former student reports, however, the so-called "Lost Generation" enjoyed social privilege as well as literary fame and the greedy, corrupt, self-deluded, morally and ethically bankrupt Americans they wrote about represented an extremely small percentage of the American population at that time. Who, the student asks, really were the "lost generation"?

> In all likelihood, they were middle class whites with the means and the social privilege that allowed them to be "disillusioned" .... Did all Americans in the Twenties drive home from their high-paying jobs in Model-T Fords, stopping to buy a few stocks and the latest George Gershwin record before proceeding home in time to catch the latest episode of "Amos 'n' Andy"? What was the 'other' America going through at this time? Working and living conditions for the poor were awful: 25,000 were killed on the job each year and 100,000 were permanently disabled ... two million people in New York City 'lived in

---

[4] From a March, 1992, report submitted by an eleventh-grade student, Nicholas Rosenburg.

tenements condemned as firetraps.' Bitter strikes broke out among
railroad workers .... (Zinn 375). Distrust of foreigners, combined with
long-standing hatred toward minorities, led to the reviving of the Klu
Klux Klan; more than two million Americans joined the secret
organization to terrorize foreigners, Blacks, Jews, and Roman Catholics
(Cronon 33 9-341).[5]

Section D.4: Sample Interrogation Questions

Do not ask the text questions it obviously expects or solicits from you as a
specialist in its language; ask questions as utterly alien to its experience,
lifestyle, and literary reputation as you can imagine. Following are some
questions which other interrogators have found useful but the best
inquiries follow from your own "take" on the text. (For more ideas, watch
media detectives Columbo and Poirot in action. As interrogators of "high
class," texts, they are superb.)

* Precisely where does this text least expect to be questioned?

* Who are the people this text loves to hate? To what groups, ideas,
  behaviors, cultural practices is it openly hostile?

* What kinds of texts would this text enjoy? What are its sexual,
  literary, social, cultural preferences?

* What behaviors does this text feel comfortable condemning? What
  sorts of punishments can it safely recommend?

* What uses of itself would this text enjoy? What subtitles would it
  approve, even appreciate?

* What does this text think of *you*? Who would feel most
  uncomfortable reading this text? Least uncomfortable?

* What power-plays does this text deploy with impunity and what
  ideas-at-large protect it?

* Who writes on the back cover of this text? On the inside flap?
  Who recommends it?

* What individuals or institutions does this text acknowledge and
  thank? What grants and public funds have supported it?

---

[5] From a March, 1992, report submitted by an eleventh-grade student, Matthew Biel.

* Do the "facts" of the text's publishing history include changes? How do you account for them?

* What is the appeal of the text's cover? To whom is it addressed?

As you can see, the above questions do not inquire of a text's deep, secret "meaning"; they probe its culture connections. The new historicist interrogation is not focused on the "author" or the text as an art-object, but on the discourse that links the text with the politics and culture of its time period.

THIS MANUAL IS THE PROPERTY OF PRECINCT 101.
IT MAY NOT BE DISTRIBUTED TO UNAUTHORIZED PERSONNEL
EXCEPT BY PERMISSION OF THE PRECINCT CAPTAIN.

References

Arnold, Judy and Benjamin S. Howard. "The Structuralist Student in a Post-Structuralist Age." *Conversations: Contemporary Critical Theory and the Teaching of Literature.* Eds. Charles Moran and Elizabeth F. Penfield. Urbana, Illinois: NCTE, 1990. 164-178.

Barthes, Roland. *The Pleasure of the Text.* Trans. Richard Miller. 1973; New York: Hill and Wang, 1975.

Barthes, Roland. *Roland Barthes.* Trans. Richard Howard. New York: Hill and Wang, 1977.

Booth, Wayne. "The Rhetorical Stance." *The Writing Teacher's Sourcebook.* Eds. Gary Tate and Edward P. J. Corbett. 1963; New York: Oxford UP, 1981. 108-116.

Booth, Wayne. *The Vocation of a Teacher: Rhetorical Occasions.* Chicago: U of Chicago P, 1989.

Bourdieu, Pierre. *Distinction: A Social Critique of the Judgement of Taste.* Trans. Richard Nice. 1979; Cambridge: Harvard UP, 1984.

Bourdieu, Pierre & Jean-Claude Passeron. *Reproduction in Education, Society and Culture.* Trans. Richard Nice. 1977; London: Sage Publications, 1990.

Bove, Paul A. "Foreward the Foucault Phenomenon: The Problematics of Style." In *Foucault* by Gilles Deleuze: vii-xl.

Brooks, Cleanth. *The Well Wrought Urn.* Harcourt, Brace and Company: New York, 1947.

Brown, Bruce and Ralph Gaillard, Jr. "Decade." *Washington Post* 13 December 1989: 20.

Byatt, A. S. *Possession: A Romance.* New York: Random House, 1990.

Cahalan, James M. and David B. Downing, eds. *Practicing Theory in Introductory College Literature Courses,* (NCTE: Urbana, 1991).

Caramello, Charles. "On 'Word Rain', Its Equilibrium." *A Critical (Ninth) Assembling.* Ed. Richard Kostelanetz. New York: Assembling Press, 1979. N. pag.

Carroll, Lewis. *The Annotated Alice: Alice's Adventures in Wonderland & Through the Looking Glass.* New York: The World Publishing Company, 1963.

Chelifer. "The Ideas of Emily Dickinson." *Godey's Magazine* CXXXIII (July to December, 1986): 541-543.

Ciardi, John. "Robert Frost: The Way to the Poem." *Edge of Awareness: 25 Contemporary Essays.* Eds. Ned E. Hoopes and Richard Peck. New York: Dell Publishing Co., Inc., 1966. 145-155.

Craig, Hardin. *The Complete Works of Shakespeare.* Ed. Hardin Craig. New York: Scott, Foresman and Company, 1961.

Cronon, David E. "Roaring Twenties." *World Book Encyclopedia.* Volume 16, 1985.

Crowley, Sharon. *A Teacher's Introduction to Deconstruction.* NCTE Teacher's Introduction Series. Urbana, ILL.: NCTE, 1989.

Deleuze, Gilles. *Foucault*. Trans. Sean Hand. 1986; Minneapolis, Univ of Minnesota Press, 1988.

Deleuze, Gilles. In "Intellectuals and Power: A Conversation between Michel Foucault and Gilles Deleuze." *Language, Counter-Memory, Practice: Selected Essays and Interviews by Michel Foucault*. Ed. Donald F. Bouchard. Ithaca: Cornell UP, 1977. 205-217.

Derrida, Jacques. "An Interview with Derrida." Trans. David Allison. *Derrida and Différance*. Eds. David Wood and Robert Bernasconi. 1985; Evanston, Illinois: Northwestern UP, 1988. 71-82.

Derrida, Jacques. *Différance*. Trans. by Alan Bass. *Margins of Philosophy*. Chicago: University of Chicago Press, 1982.

Derrida, Jacques. *Dissemination*. Trans. Barbara Johnson. 1972; Chicago: U of Chicago P, 1981.

Derrida, Jacques. Of Grammatology. Trans. Gayatri Spivak. 1967; Baltimore: Johns Hopkins UP, 1976. Cited in the text as *OG*.

Derrida, Jacques. *Positions*. Trans. Alan Bass. Chicago, Illinois: Univ. of Chicago P, 1981.

Derrida, Jacques. *The Post Card: From Socrates to Freud and Beyond*. Trans. Alan Bass. 1980; Chicago: U of Chicago P, 1987.

Derrida, Jacques. "The Purveyor of Truth." *The Purloined Poe: Lacan, Derrida, and Psychoanalytic Reading*. Ed. John P. Muller and William J. Richardson. Trans. Alan Bass. Baltimore: The Johns Hopkins Univ. Press, 1988. 173-212.

Dreyfus, Hubert L. and Paul Rabinow. *Michel Foucault: Beyond Structuralism and Hermeneutics.* 2nd Ed. Chicago: U of Chicago P, 1983. 1-16.

Dunlop, M. H. "Practicing Textual Theory and Teaching Formula Fiction." *Practicing Theory in Introductory College Literature Courses.* Ed. James M. Cahalan and David B. Downing. Urbana, Illinois: NCTE, 1991: 251- 260.

Emig, Janet. "Our Missing Theory." *Conversations: Contemporary Critical Theory and the Teaching of Literature.* Eds. Charles Moran and Elizabeth F. Penfield; NCTE, 1990. 87-96.

Federman, Raymond. "Surfiction—Four Propositions in Form of an Introduction." *Surfiction: Fiction Now... and tomorrow.* Ed. Raymond Federman. Chicago: Swallow Press, 1975: 5-15.

Fitzgerald, F. Scott. *The Great Gatsby.* New York: Macmillan Publishing Company, 1980.

Fish, Stanley. "Commentary: The Young and the Restless." *The New Historicism.* Ed. H. Aram Veeser. Routledge: New York, 1989. 303-316.

Foucault, Michel. "Afterward: The Subject and Power." *Michel Foucault: Beyond Structuralism and Hermeneutics.* Ed. Hubert L. Dreyfus and Paul Rabinow. Chicago: Univ of Chicago P, 1983. 208-226.

Foucault, Michel. "The Confession of the Flesh." *Power/Knowledge: Selected Interviews & Other Writings 1972-1977.* Ed. Colin Gordon. New York: Pantheon Books, 1980. 194-228.

Foucault, Michel. *Discipline and Punish.* Trans. Alan Sheridan 1975; New York: Vintage Books, 1979.

Foucault, Michel. "The Discourse on Language." *The Archaeology of Knowledge & the Discourse on Language.* Trans. A. M. Sheridan Smith. 1971; New York: Pantheon Books, 1972. 215-237.

Foucault, Michel. "The Ethic of Care for the Self as a Practice of Freedom." Trans. j. d. gauthier, s.j. *The Final Foucault.* Eds. James Bernauer and David Rasmussen. 1987; Cambridge: MIT Press, 1988. 1-20.

Foucault, Michel. *The History of Sexuality, Volume I: An Introduction.* 1976; New York: Vintage Books, 1980.

Foucault, Michel. "On the Genealogy of Ethics: An Overview of Work in Progress." Found in op.cit *Michel Foucault: Beyond Structuralism and Hermeneutics.* By Hubert L. Dreyfus and Paul Rabinow. 229-252.

Foucault, Michel. "Intellectuals and Power: A conversation between Michel Foucault and Gilles Deleuze." *Language, Counter Memory, Practice: Selected Essays and Interviews.* Ed. Donald F. Bouchard. Trans. Donald F. Bouchard and Sherry Simon. Ithaca: Cornell UP, 1977.

Foucault, Michel. "The Politics of Health in the Eighteenth Century." *Power/Knowledge: Selected Interviews & Other Writings 1972-1977.* Ed. Colin Gordon. New York: Pantheon Books, 1980. 166-182.

Foucault, Michel. "Revolutionary Action: 'Until Now' A discussion with Michel Foucault under the auspices of *Actuel*" Found in op.cit *Language, CounterMemory, Practice: Selected Essays and Interviews.* Ed. Donald F. Bouchard. Trans. Donald F. Bouchard and Sherry Simon. Ithaca: Cornell UP, 1977. 218-233.

Foucault, Michel. "The Subject and Power." Afterword. Found in op.cit *Michel Foucault: Beyond Structuralism and Hermeneutics*. By Hubert L. Dreyfus and Paul Rabinow. 208-226.

Foucault, Michel. "Two Lectures." *Power/ Knowledge: Selected Interviews & Other Writings 1972-1977*. Ed. Colin Gordon. Trans. by Colin Gordon, Leon Marshall, John Mepham, Kate Soper. New York: Pantheon Books, 1980. 78-108.

Foucault, Michel. "Questions on Geography." *Power/Knowledge: Selected Interviews & Other Writings 1972-1977*. Ed. Colin Gordon. New York: Pantheon Books, 1980. 63-77.

Gins, Madeline. *Word Rain or A Discursive Introduction to The Intimate Philosophical Investigations of G,R,E,T,A, G,A,R,B,O, It Says*. New York: Grossman Publishers, 1969.

Giroux, Henry A. "Liberal Arts Education and the Struggle for Public Life: Dreaming about Democracy." *The Politics of Liberal Education*. Eds Darryl J. Gless and Barbara Herrnstein Smith. Durham: Duke Univ. Press, 1992: 119-144.

Gore, Al. "Networking the Future." Washington Post 15 July 1990: B3.

Greenblatt, Stephen. "Culture." *Critical Terms for Literary Study*. Ed. Frank Lentricchia and Thomas McLaughlin. Chicago: Univ. of Chicago Press, 1990: 225-232.

Greenblatt, Stephen. *Renaissance Self-Fashionino: From More to Shakespeare*. Chicago: Univ of Chicago Press, 1980. Orig. in "Of the new lands", in *The First Three English Books on America*, ed. Edward Arber (Birmingham. Turnbull and Spears, 1995), p. xxvii.

Greenblatt, Stephen. "Towards a Poetics of Culture." *The New Historicism*. Ed. H. Aram Veeser. New York: Routledge, 1989. 1-14.

Grumet, Madeleine R. *Bitter Milk: Women and Teaching*. Amherst: The Univ. of Massachusetts Press, 1988.

Habermas, Jürgen. "Taking Aim at the Heart of the Present." *Foucault: A Critical Reader*. Ed. David Couzens Hoy. New York: Basil Blackwell Inc., 1986. 103-108.

Hacking, Ian. "The Archaeology of Foucault." *Foucault: A Critical Reader*. Ed. David Couzens Hoy. New York: Basil Blackwell Inc., 1986. 27-40.

Hand, Sean. "Translating Theory." In *Foucault*, by Gilles Deleuze. Minneapolis, Univ. of Minnesota Press: 1988. xli- xliv.

Hoy, David Couzens. "Power, Repression, Progress." *Foucault: A Critical Reader*, ed. David Couzens Hoy. Basil Blackwall: New York, 1986. 123-147.

Johnson, Barbara, ed. *The Pedagogical Imperative: Teaching as a Literary Genre*. Yale French Studies No. 63 (1982).

Kael, Pauline. "Stonework." Rev. of *Dead Poets Society*. *New Yorker* 26 June 1989: 70-71.

Kesey, Ken. *One Flew Over the Cuckoo's Nest*. New York, The Viking Press, 1962.

Kristeva, Julia. *Desire in Language: A Semiotic Approach to Literature and Art*. Ed. Leon S. Roudiez. Trans. Thomas Gora, Alice Jardine, and Leon S. Roudiez. 1977; New York: Columbia P, 1980.

Kristeva, Julia. *Revolution in Poetic Language*. Trans. Margaret Waller. 1974; New York: Columbia UP, 1984.

LaGrandeur, Kevin. "Aporia and the Emptied Teacher: Deconstruction and the Unraveling of (Con) 'Texts.'" *Literary Theory in the Classroom* 18.2 (1991): 69-79.

Leitch, Vincent B. "Deconstruction and Pedagogy." *Theory in the Classroom*. Ed. Cary Nelson. Urbana: U of Illinois P, 1986. 45-56.

Lorca, Federico Garcia. "Somnarnbulistic Ballad," in *Focus on Literature: Ideas*. ed. Philip McFarland et al. Boston: Houghton Mifflin Company, 1978): 346-348.

Marius, Richard. "A Common Ground: The Essay in the Academy." *College English* 51 (1989): Montefiore, 262-276.

Montefiore, Jan. *Feminism and Poetry: Language, Experience, Identity in Women's Writing*. New York: Pandora, 1987.

Perrine, Laurence, ed. *Literature: Sound, Structure, and Sense*, Fifth Edition. New York: Harcourt Brace Jovanovich, Inc., 1989.

Poster, Mark. "Foucault and the Tyranny of Greece." *Foucault: A Critical Reader*. Ed. David Couzens Hoy. New York: Basil Blackwell Inc., 1986. Rich, 205-220.

Rich, Adrienne. "Frame." *A Wild Patience Has Taken Me This Far: Poems 1978-1981*. New York: W. W. Norton & Co.,1981. 46-48.

Rich, Adrienne. "Integrity." *A Wild Patience ...* 8-9.

Rich, Adrienne. "Readings of History." *Snapshots of a Daughter-in-Law: Poems 1954-1962*. New York, W.W. Norton & Co., 1967.

Rich, Adrienne. "Upper Broadway." *The Dream of a Common Language: Poems 1974-1977.* New York: W.W. Norton & Co., 1978.

Rich, Adrienne. "Tear Gas." *The Fact of a Doorframe: Poems Selected —and New 1950-1984.* New York: W.W. Norton & Company, 1984. 198-200.

Richter, David H. ed. *The Critical Tradition: Classic Texts and Contemporary Trends.* New York: St. Martin's Press, 1989.

Said, Edward W. *The World, the Text, and the Critic.* Cambridge: Harvard UP, 1983.

Scholes, Robert. "Toward a Curriculum in Textual Studies." *Reorientations: Critical Theories & Pedagogies.* Eds. Bruce Henricksen and Thais E. Morgan. Urbana: U of Illinois P, 1990. 95-111.

Spivak, Gayatri Chakravorty. "Political Commitment and the Postmodern Critic." *The New Historicism.* Ed. H. Aram Veeser. New York: Routledge, 1989. 277-292.

"The New World and the New Man." *The Atlantic Monthly: A Magazine of Literature, Art, and Politics."* II (October, 1858): 515-531.

Thomas, Brook. "The Historical Necessity for – and Difficulties with – New Historical Analysis in Introductory Literature Courses." *Practicing Theory in Introductory College Literature Courses.* Ed. James M. Cahalan and David B. Downing. Urbana, Illinois: NCTE, 1991. 85-100.

Thomas, Brook. "The New Historicism and other Old-fashioned Topics." *The New Historicism.* Ed. H. Aram Veeser. New York: Routlege, 1989. 182-203.

Thompkins, Jane. "Pedagogy of the Distressed." *College English* 52 (1990): 653-660.

Treichler, Paula A. "Teaching Feminist Theory." *Theory in the Classroom.* Ed. Cary Nelson. Urbana: U Illinois P, 1986. 57-128.

Ulmer, Gregory L. *Applied Grammatology: Post (e) – Pedagogy from Jacques Derrida to Joseph Beuys.* Baltimore: Johns Hopkins University Press, 1985. Cited in the text as AG.

Ulmer, Gregory L. *Teletheory.* New York: Routledge, 1989.

Ulmer, Gregory L. "Textshop for an Experimental Humanities." *Reorientations: Critical Theories and Pedagogies.* Ed. Bruce Henricksen and Thais E. Morgan. Urbana, Illinois: U of Illinois P, 1990: 113-132.

Ulmer, Gregory L. "Textshop for Psychoanalysis: On De-Programming Freshmen Platonists." *College English* 49 (1987): 756-769.

Vesser, H. Aram, ed. "Introduction." *The New Historicism,* ed. H. Aram Vesser. Routledge: New York, 1989. ix-xvi.

Widick, Carole, L. Lee Knefelkamp, Clyde A. Parker. "The Counselor as a Developmental Instructor." *Counselor Education and Supervision* 14. (1975): 286-296.

Zavarzadeh, Mas'ud and Donald Morton. "(Post) modern Critical Theory and the Articulations of Critical Pedagogies." *College Literature* 17 (1990): 51-63.

Zavarzadeh, Mas'ud and Donald Morton. "Theory Pedagogy Politics: The Crisis of 'The Subject' in the Humanities." *Texts for Change: Theory/Pedagogy/Politics*. Eds. Donald Morton and Mas'ud Zavarzadeh. Urbana, Illinois: U of Illinois P, 1991. 1-32.

Zinn, Howard. *A People's History of the United States*. New York: Harper and Row, 1980.

`

Index

Dedication

This book was written by my mother who taught English for 37 years in nine states, receiving many awards for high school teaching, including the Maryland Teacher of the Year Award in 1985.

She went back to school in her late 50's to earn her doctorate in English Literature, which she completed at the University of Maryland, College Park in 1991. In her college teaching she was recognized for expertise in postmodern theory and was a master teacher in a training program at the University of Maryland.

She died in 1997, before this book[1], which is based on her dissertation, could be published.

One of my biggest regrets is that I didn't read her dissertation then— probably because I didn't understand it. I majored in history and saw postmodernism as ahistorical and non-political. I had read Derrida and Foucault, but it was only after I had unearthed and read a draft copy of her dissertation that I began to really understand these theorists.

I was amazed by the way she broke down the fundamental theories of these two towering figures in postmodern theory. In the core of this book, she applied them to teaching high school English, and teaching in general, with humor, playfulness, remarkable ingenuity and creativity.

As I read various sections of her dissertation, I was overcome by emotion and with my memories of her as a unique mother, teacher and academic. While pursuing her doctorate in the late 1980's as she taught full-time, she was drawn to postmodern theory and began to incorporate what she was learning into her classroom.

Her students were always central to her pedagogy and many dinner table conversations were peppered with how she incorporated her students' perspectives, music, culture and spirit into her lesson plans (in fact, the title of this book, "Killer English," comes from a comment on

---

[1] This book is what I believe to be the last edited version of what she was shopping to prospective publishers right before her death – It was a printed manuscript of her Preface, Introduction, Chapters 1-5, the Appendices and her References. I didn't have the computer files, so I had to use OCR to get it into a Word document, and I created a Table of Contents. I hired freelancers to complete the rest of the work.

one of her student evaluations: "the class was 'Killer,' meaning "excellent," in the slang of the time).

Born in 1935, my mother had a very traditional English literature education, steeped in the Norton Anthology, New Criticism, Northrup Frye, etc. In her time at College Park, she attended many conferences on theory. She told me a story about being "backstage" at a conference with Umberto Eco, who was sitting on a couch smoking a cigarette. Since he was sitting alone, one of her colleagues, who knew my mom also smoked, encouraged her to sit down and have a cigarette with him. A little starstruck, she sat down and when she lit up, Eco told her not to worry because "in Italy they have developed a cigarette with no cholesterol!"

In June 2022 I reached out to the person who was closest to my mom while she was on her intellectual journey through postmodern theory. I found her principal doctoral advisor, Susan Handelman, and we spontaneously exchanged many emails, reflecting on my mother's life and work. In those correspondences, she strongly encouraged me to self-publish the dissertation and "just get it out there!"

Now, just over two years later and after many fits and starts, I am finally getting it 'out there.'

This book is dedicated to her memory.

——

There are many people who were indispensable to making this book happen:

First, my father, Frank Delia, who encouraged me to persevere throughout this daunting process, from digitizing the paper manuscript all the way to the final product (I found out quickly that it takes a while to find honest brokers in the self-publishing world!).

Erica Cosentino, a free-lancer editor I found on-line, captured some of the changes that have occurred in the field and how this work might inform them. You will find her thoughtful comments peppered throughout in various footnotes after the [Ed.] symbol.

Ernesto Mora, (eamora2012@gmail.com, freelancer.com/u/eamora2014) another free-lancer who did an absolute fantastic job formatting and laying out the entire book.

Amron Lehte, at Wild Clover Book Services, who performed an exceptional task in putting together the index.

Susan Lanser for her beautifully written Foreword that truly captured the essence of the book and its on-going relevance to the ever-expanding field of critical pedagogy.

And finally, to Susan Handelman, who without her encouragement and guidance this project might never have come about. Her utterly moving Afterword, with her memories and stories about my mother, as well as our personal correspondences, have help me appreciate just how special and unique my mother's gifts truly were.

———

It would be wonderful if this book found its way into the hands of some of Mary's Alice's former students, colleagues, or acquaintances. I have set up a website to welcome any and all comments, thoughts, or perspectives about the book: www.postmodernpedagogy.com.

All proceeds from the sale of this book will be donated to the Human Restoration Project, a 501(c)3 nonprofit that promotes, among other things, progressive education and critical pedagogy in the United States and across the globe.

Joseph Delia
josephbdelia@gmail.com
October 2024

www.ingramcontent.com/pod-product-compliance
Lightning Source LLC
Chambersburg PA
CBHW051304120626
46547CB00015B/2082